Other Works by This Author

The 4 Secrets of the Universe

All About the Soul's Journey

The Book of Manifesting

Mysteries, Prophecies, and the Hollow Earth

The Lightness of Being

Sojourn

Poet Gone Wild

Poems of Life, Love, and the Meaning of Meaning

Infinite Healing

Poems and Messages for the Loss of a Loved One

Poems and Messages for the Loss of Your Animal Companion

The 5th Secret

In the Universe that I Am

PAUL GORMAN

Copyright © 2025 Paul J. Gorman
All Rights Reserved

Year of the Book
135 Glen Avenue
Glen Rock, PA 17327

ISBN 13: 978-1-64649-494-1 (print)
ISBN 13: 978-1-64649-495-8 (ebook)

Cover photo by author, Western Maryland
Additional photos licensed from Alamy and Shutterstock.

No part of this publication may be reproduced, distributed, or transmitted in any form or by any means, including photocopying, recording, or other electronic or mechanical methods, without the prior written permission of the author, except in the case of brief quotations embodied in critical reviews and certain other noncommercial uses permitted by copyright law.

Library of Congress Control Number: 2025906471

Disclaimer:
This book contains spiritual messages and information, recommendations and insights. It does not contain financial or medical advice.

Any predictions discussed are meaningless because of the interactive nature of our individual universes. Each person creates their own future every moment.

I do not favor one particular religion, country, or political party—only peace and well-being for all people, and for all of life. In my opinion, there are no political solutions, only personal solutions.

I am also not opposed to the use of profanity, when used for emphasis in a harmless, 'George Carlin kind of way'. The only profanity in this book happens to be in the message from the late comedian, George Carlin.

Some names have been altered for privacy.

Contents

Foreword 1
Introduction 2
John Candy 7
Bob Newhart 10
Freddie Mercury 13
David Bowie 17
George Harrison 23
John Lennon 27
Dr. Martin Luther King, Jr. 33
Wolfgang Mozart 38
Vincent Van Gogh 41
St. Francis of Assisi 44
Constanza 46
BJ
   1: An Astral Individuation 48
   2: The 5th Secret 50
   3: Here I Am 52
   4: A Blue Screen 55
   5: All That There Is 57
   6: An Imaginary Dream 59
   7: A Lifetime to Find Healing In 61
   8: No Timelines Exist 64
   9: Dying to Heal 65
   10: Ecstasy and Expansiveness 67
   11: A Council of Elders 69
Amelia Earhart 72
The Voynich Manuscript 75
Roswell, NM 79

The Mary Celeste 81
A New Year 85
A Free Energy Machine 88
Peppers and Cancer 90
Two Dream Meanings 93
The Rest of the Sentence 95
Baron B.
   1: Allowing Love is God 96
   2: Nothing to Need 99
   3: Find a Common Denomination 102
   4: You Are God 103
   5: The Most Delightful Incarnation 106
   6: Self-Forgiveness Mantra 108
   7: A Steady Rate of Ascension 110
   8: The Endgame Dream 113
   9: The 6th Secret 114
   Note to Self
Dave C.
   1: Enormous Implications 117
   2: No Darkness or Shadows in It 119
Teen Suicide 124
Loriann 132
Messages to Family Members 138
Sam N. 141
An Angel of Kindness 144
Paul P. 146
Colin M. 148
Doc 151
Mack 156
Entity Attachments 160
Andrew and Jay 162

Raymond Toy C...166
Golgatha 167
Sold Their Souls 172
Saint Germain 173
Hillo..177
Ivols
   1: Being God-Like 182
   2: Perpetuates God Mind in Eternity 184
Byron Manning 187
Highly Evolved Beings and the Light of Jesus ...190
Bijil..194
A Soul Director...197
Leroy 201
   Myself I Met 205
An Instant of Recognition................................. 208
Shadow.. 211
   As Good As You 212
   Truly Alive...215
Cali 216
Rocco 217
The Buffer Zone 219
Anthoula A.
   1: The Only Requirement 222
   2: In 4 Different Centuries...........................225
A Doom Loop 229
Edgar Cayce 236
Michelle L... 243
Angel Death... 246
Admiral Richard Byrd.. 249
Lulo
   1: The Inner-Earth 254

    2: Intrusions into the Inner-Earth 257
    3: Civilization Inside the Earth 262
    4: A Merkabah 264
    Healed in God Mind Instantly
    5: Return to the Surface 269
    6: Ala 271
Robert 276
Abundance 278
John S. 281
Chris T. 284
Nostradamus
    1: Awareness Is a Choice 287
    I Know – You Know
    2: Finding Meaning 290
    Each of Us
The 5 Energies Adversely Affecting Humanity .. 294
    My Moment With You
Being a Light Being 300
Marty
    1: In an Instant Moment 304
    2: Only One Point of Reference 308
    3: As God Yourself 311
It Will Disappear 314
More Time, Or Not 316
The Top 5 Things 318
Exposing the Lie 319
Archangel Gabriel 321
The Most Important Chapter 324
Archangel Raphael 328
Jimmy Stewart 332
Gene Hackman 334

Donald Sutherland	336
Bob Hope	341
Groucho Marx	342
George Burns	344
Leslie Nielsen	345
George Carlin	347
You Bet Your Life After Death	351
Bashar	357
A Boom Loop	360
I Am One Too	364
Afterword	366
Postscript	367
Affirmations	368

Foreword

The 5th Secret: In the Universe that I Am explores the spirit world through channeled messages from God, the light of Jesus, ascended masters, archangels, angels, the Council of Elders, and people who have died—including well-known historical figures, artists, musicians, comedic actors and a courageous civil rights leader.

The conversations also explore spiritual concepts, previously unexplained mysteries, the inner-earth, and more importantly, it discusses how we can live more effectively in our day-to-day lives. It was written in late 2024 into early 2025, after the publication of *All About the Soul's Journey: Understanding Death,* and *The 4 Secrets of the Universe*: *Making the 'You' in Universe.*

I wanted to know more about the spirit world, and what it is really like. Is it possible for us to be here, and not there?

Maybe in a dream. Why are we here now?

We are always here now. Where is that, exactly? How could that be?

Introduction

The chances of your being here, and at this time, are one in many trillions. The odds are calculated by multiplying the variables together. For our lifetime incarnations, I understand that there are hundreds of planets to choose from as a human being, with an almost unlimited number of locations, and an infinite number of time periods in different timelines.

That alone should give us pause to consider our uniqueness, and the perfection that went into our being right here, right now. We are not here by chance, but by choice.

If you believe that we are infinite consciousness, with free will—then it means we specifically chose our lifetimes—including our families, or not—and our major lifetime challenges. We were then born to keep on choosing.

Why do we choose our lifetime circumstances? To learn from them, and to heal in them. Life only asks us to respond to our chosen challenges with courage. These achievements are then entrained into our souls. How do we heal in them? By choosing responses that will heal them—in our minds. Healing responses are kind and loving thoughts. Having kind and loving thoughts about ourselves and others makes us one with God in those moments. Can we be one with God? That is the goal of life—and also its outcome. Why not bring the outcome to the present? That is where it exists—and the only place it can exist.

My messages say that if I find things in life to despise, that makes me a despiser. If I find things to hate, the hate is only in my mind. It will certainly not raise my consciousness, or make me one with God in those moments. Actually, it will have the opposite effect of manifesting what I do not want by disabling my ability to manifest goodness. My free will is always choosing. It is choosing what my mind will then create.

The universe teaches me in a feedback loop, either positive or negative—directed by my thoughts. I create it by projecting it, and I project it to learn from it. The universe is a perfect reflector of what is in my mind. It allows me to advance in consciousness or not, however I choose to. If choosing kind and loving thoughts makes me one with God, then as one with God I could only create a positive feedback loop to live in. I can imagine what a negative feedback loop in my mind would create, or miscreate in my life.

Do you recall ever having a perfect day—a day of synchronicities, and of always being in the right place at the right time—where even setbacks worked in your favor? Every day can unfold that way.

Is it possible for kind and loving thoughts, or God, to create a negative feedback loop? How could choosing to be one with God now, not create a perfect day?

That is the theme of my books. I wanted to know—how does the universe work? How can I prosper and not suffer?

You can program your energy field to allow only love and goodness into it. Love and goodness are what God is, and only exist in the present moment, always now. Allowing only love and goodness into your mind, and your life, means that a lot of circumstances and people will not be joining you. Prepare yourself for it. They will not be looped into your perfect days.

The 5th Secret: In the Universe that I Am continues the exploration of consciousness, with many chapters of insight and advice from the spirit world that supports us. The chapters were written during a period of major transition in the world.

The outer world is always in transition—spinning, transiting, circling, and expanding.

How do we navigate through everything that is always in motion? It is in motion for us to loop into it, or out of it—giving us constant feedback on whether or not we are perpetuating a positive loop, or a negative loop. It depends on the healed or unhealed thoughts that we are choosing.

Having free will to choose makes us 100% responsible for our own universes, and only our own. Do I want to live in a godly or an ungodly universe? It depends on what I choose to think.... and only "I." Others cannot manifest for us, nor us for them.

You do not have to participate in the ungodly side of life's illusion. It is only there for you to choose what you desire to create more of.

Many people have lives that are very challenging. I often think that the more challenging a person's life is, the more advanced their soul could be to have set the bar so high. They set it high to find the courage, strength, and love within themselves to rise to the challenges. The goal is not to necessarily overcome the challenges, but "to find the courage, strength, and love within themselves," which is God.

The messages that I received in this book are from God Mind, and from communications with different entities that I am addressing.

Here is a message from God Mind which is from the chapter "The 5 Energies Adversely Affecting Humanity":

> *"Achievement in life means halting all non-loving thoughts. It heals your mind, and manifests your desires.*
>
> *How can a healed projection not be all that you desire it to be? It cannot be anything other than what is most advantageous for your soul."*

Note that in this exploration of consciousness—life and afterlife, past and future, reality and illusion, time and timelessness—that the topic of 'end times' is discussed in several chapters. The last chapters explain how it is possible to not loop into it.

"For life and death are one, and only those who will consider the experience as one may come to understand or comprehend what peace indeed means."

—Edgar Cayce

John Candy

Can I please speak with John Candy?
Actually, you have been speaking with him for a while now, as he hears you laughing at his funniest movie and TV scenes.

Hi John, I would like to have met you. Steve Martin said you were very kind—in an interview about your month together filming *Planes, Trains, and Automobiles*.
Don't believe him—he is a comedian wanting a laugh.

Ha, ha, ha!
He always laughed at my attempts at being funny, and laughed at himself mostly for allowing himself to not be a serious writer.

Did Steve want to be a serious writer?
He had the ability and talent, but always had another funny comedy going on in his head.

Did you achieve your lifetime dreams? Maybe I should say "goals" since life is a dream.
A lifetime is a dream with only 4 components. All 4 are comedic in nature.
First, a male has intercourse with a female, and you are conceived.
Second, you arrive coming out of the female at her nether region.
Third, all you have to do is love, even if you do not get love.

And fourth—here is the big one—all will heal if you allow yourself a moment of escape from the dream.

Was your lifespan determined before you were born?

It had a beginning and an ending that were determined before I chose the life to heal in.

Did you heal in life?

I healed all that I could, meaning all of the insecurities that I had about myself.

Can you please tell me what dying was like?

All healing, all knowing, all exhilaration, and all ecstasy in having God's love incredibly illuminate your mind.

Did an angel visit you before you died?

"Am I dead?" is what I said to the angel because I was asleep. All I could feel was an incredible light in my mind. The angel asked me if I was ready to go with it to another place that all comedic actors go to.

I followed and asked if it was a clown world where I was not allowed a costume.

It said that I would see, and could decide if I needed one. After that, I said I needed one.

It gave me one with an orange wig and a red nose, and said, "Let's go meet God."

Haaa, haaa, haaa!

It gets better because God had on the same costume that I did, and we were identical.

At that moment, I realized I was God having a dream.

Then what happened?

I had an introspection period where I reviewed my life as a clown, having a dream to clown around in. It could have been better, and it could have been worse, but I did okay—but didn't love myself as much as I could have.

Everyone loved you here.
All love heals me in their thoughts when they see me in their minds.

What would you like to say to people now?
All God has in store for you is already inside of you—and the costume comes with it.

Bob Newhart

Hi Bob!
Actually, I am not a psychologist... hear, hear me out on this... I am a comedian that died in one last ha-ha-ha... and had the last laugh, because it was funny to me.

How was it funny?
Before I died, I said that I had to go eat something. After eating a lot of the meal, I died. After dying, I found it comical to eat something and die.

That is comical—and very fitting for your observational comedy and dead-pan style, yuk, yuk.
Actually, I didn't really die, but people believe I did. I am a comedian, acting like it was funny to live and die in a comedy—acting that it cannot be a tragedy, only a comedy that you alone can find the humor in. Acting like it is not a comedy does not have the intended effect.

You made many millions of people laugh, and see the humor in life.
All I could do was laugh inside in the same moments because each moment has its humor to observe.

What was it like to die?
It allowed me to feel how all of the books said I would feel.

An incredible brightness exploded in my head and held me in it until I started moving out of my body. All I could feel was exhilaration.

After I left my body, an angelic being and another being that had been my guide on Earth, he said, guided me higher in consciousness, and away from the Earth.

All I could feel was healed in an indescribable and all-encompassing lovingness.

Where did you go?
Actually, all I could do was laugh at my eating and dying at that moment, and then all of us ascended to where all comedic actors go—and actors that are not comedic are not allowed.

They have to watch and understand so they can learn how to act.

Ha, ha!
Comedic acting allows actors to improvise, but the timing has to be perfect.

Acting in comedies has almost no comparison for creating a lot of joy in the world.

You certainly did that.
I did that, and I didn't do that. The joy was inside of each person waiting for a reason to come out.

Great point. They can see the beauty and humor all the time, and just let the joy out.
Exactly, and I'm not a psychologist... hear, hear me out on this...

Ha, ha! I send you love from the Earth where you brought out so much joy.
I'm going to get something to eat...

Haaa, haaa!
I... I didn't get to the funny part yet...

Freddie Mercury

Can I speak with Freddie Mercury?

Freddie illuminates here, and will illuminate in your head, and in your writing.

Hello Freddie!

Freddie, as I was known in life, is not so flamboyant now. All I can do is have a 'Crazy Little Thing Called Love'.

Great song.

It heals in my mind when I need it to.

What have you been doing since you died?

I always go into a healing classroom when I allow myself another helpful instruction on how I could have loved myself more than I did in life.

Please tell me about the classrooms.

All have a blackboard and a desk for the class instructor—and all have either one student, or many students.
'Healing' is always the course description.

Is your assignment on the blackboard?

I always have an assignment written on it.

What is your assignment?

On the blackboard it says I have a homework assignment. It has my name, and lists 8 items next to it.

#1 "Can healing be infinite, or can it be finished in healing your mind?"

Number one has another part to it. It says, "List how healing can be infinite or finished."

#2 "Can God have healing, or is God healed?", and "Can God heal what is not healed?"

#3 "All God healing can be illuminated in what manner, and in what life forms?"

#4 "How can God heal me, and how can I heal myself?"

#5 "How am I God, and how can I not be God?"

Number 5 has another part, "How can God not be me?"

Number 5 has a lot more to it that is incidental to the main questions. Number 5 could be my biggest challenge here.

#6 "How could I be God and hear myself talking if I am all that there is?"

#7 "How can all that there is be God having a conversation with a being that is part of all that there is?"

#8 Number 8 has another question asking, "How can I be God asking questions if I am God?"

You have some really hard questions. I don't think I could answer any of them.

Can God have a question and no answer? It is not only impossible, it is incomprehensible.

Can you tell me what it was like when you died?

All I could hear was God in my mind asking if I could come hear myself sing for it. I said, "Yes," and instantly I became what higher beings call "illuminated in God."

It healed me totally, and all I could do was have one less thing to heal—and that was my body.

I no longer had a body, and was a light being. It was magnificent, I can assure you.

An angel and a guide came to meet me, saying I was expected. After I realized I was dead, I asked both of them where we would be going. They acknowledged and answered, "We are going to God."

I acknowledged and asked, "How can we get to where God is?"

They both laughed at my question and said that I am God.

I could hardly believe it, and thought I must be having a dream. They heard my thought and said that I had just awakened from my dream.

All of a sudden, I appeared in an auditorium that had a film playing of my life. I could hear and feel everything from each person's perspective. It was an awful performance, but I had to hear and feel all of my hurtful and unloving episodes.

After all of that played, I arrived in a classroom devoid of students, and only I was in it.
I could hear myself asking what I had to do, and that is when my assignments appeared on the blackboard. It looks like I could be in eternity.

Thank you Freddie! I know you have a lot of homework, but you are missed here on Earth.

A lifetime dream can only be missed if you believe you are not all that there is.

Good point.

"All that there is" can be called a 'Crazy Little Thing Called Love'.

DAVID BOWIE

Is there a message from David Bowie? I keep hearing the song, 'Starman' in my head.
About that melody, I couldn't get it out of my head either. David Bowie, as I was known, is here and chatting with you now—not as a Starman—but as a light being that has heard you.
Achievement is all we can do in creation, allowing creativity as God a lifetime expression, namely as art in music in my case.

That was my thought—your talent, and original creativity was really cool stuff.
Actually, I was bored being in a lifetime creation of God Mind. I wanted more, and I decided to leave, allowing me to have no creative limits.

I watched a video titled, 'David Bowie—Starman: Top of the Pops—1972'. Thinking back to that time, it strikes me how totally original and ahead of your time that you were.
Achievement does not have an allowance for time. All creation allows for is healing all you can imagine, and it allows it.

I'd like to discuss what you are creating now, but first can you please tell me about your death experience 8 years ago?
Achievement in life means completing it with dignity. A death can be a creative, healing expression in God

that never ends, although it becomes an ending that you have determined for your life.

A death has a beginning, a middle, and an ending. In the beginning, it has to be in your imagining it, and allowing it as a construct in your dream.

Allowing it as a construct means it may or may not be a possibility. Allowing it in makes it even more of a construct that then has a middle and an ending. A construct middle has only one attribute, activated by your loving it or not. If you love it, then it is a loving construct. If you do not love it, then it is not a loving construct.

Let's assume you love your life's construct—all has love as its foundation.

A construct that is not loved has no foundation, making it as if it has no way to stand up—and it will not stand for long.

A construct ending can be as you determine it should be.

Although I have no body, and allowed my construct to end, I am allowing what you would call 'alternative constructs'—alternative constructs that will have an ending also. Alternative constructs can be all that you imagine, allow, and love.

Allowing love is not an alternative; not allowing it is. Alternatively, not allowing love makes an alternative to love, having no foundation. Having love is the only foundation that a construct can be supported by.

Because God is love, and everything else is illusory.

All constructed in love has God as its foundation. Non-loving constructs have alternative foundations that are not only illusory, they are allegories for the cave—meaning all have a need for the light, but they cannot be in the light.

The allegory is that the cave is a construct that cannot allow much light into it.

Are "constructs" everything we create—our thoughts and beliefs, and our lives?

A belief can be constructed from love or non-love, but it is always a construction that heals you in life—or defeats you in life.

I do not believe in non-love, defeat, or alternative foundations for my constructs in life—and even more so after having ended my lifetime construct.

Let's talk about your lifetime ending. Did you choose to have a cancer that would kill you after 18 months?

A cancer that has non-love as its foundation will eventually kill the entity that hosts it.

Would love heal a cancer?

A cancer has no foundation in love, so it would not be a construct that could last—but it could allow its host to kill itself.

How could a cancer kill its host if it is not a construct that could last?

It could have enough of an impact that the entity kills itself with the treatment options.

Eliminating cancer means having a loving treatment.

Were you visited by an angel before you died?
I had allowed cancer and its treatment to kill me because I needed an ending of my life to be in that window of time. An angel did come and have a conversation with me near the end, in my bedroom.
It accepted me for all that I had ever done, in all of my lifetime constructions.
After it left, an illumination in my head was so intense—actually, it was the most intense light I could ever imagine—and it was pulling me into it from my head.
I could not have been more amazed than when I left my body. I became a being healed in the light of God, meaning I was God's healed illumination of itself. A death heals into the light of God.
After I acknowledged that I was healed, I allowed my thoughts to be on healed constructions—all healed in the Mind of God, which allowed me to be one with God. Making all healed constructions was like being God.

How did you feel at that point?
I felt absolutely magnificent and enlightened. "Enlightened" has a meaning that cannot be described.
It cannot be described because a healed mind does not need anything, or a need to describe it.
At that healed point in my mind, I had a period of introspection that had all of my earthly actions illuminated on a screen that had me in each other person's position, hearing all that I was having them to hear.

I could feel all that they felt, and acknowledged that I could have been more loving.
Acknowledging that gave me a clearer picture of life from the soul's perspective.

What happened after that?
I actually had no other activities since then.

It sounds like you are an advanced soul, and reached enlightenment.
I can advance more, but do not need anything, having a healed mind.
A healed mind has only love illuminating in the Mind of God.

Can you give advice to readers of this book?
All God constructs are constructed from love.
All God constructs from love are all constructed in your mind.
All God constructs in your mind are all there is, making you the constructor.

Thank you, David!
There is a 'Starman', and it is God having a dream for you to heal yourself in.

George Harrison

Can I speak with George Harrison?
Actually, George has been asking for you to hear him, and he is a spirit guide of yours.

Wow—that's cool, and George was the coolest.
Acting cool and being cool are two different things. I acted cool because I couldn't be concerned with everything that was unimportant in life.

That was being cool, not acting cool.
I acted cool because I had to hide my true feelings. I didn't desire the attention all of the time, and not having any privacy ever.
Acting cool meant being in a body, and allowing what I wanted to be almost an afterthought to what the group wanted to do. I acted cool because I did not want to be cool and follow my own course—allowing all I did be what the group wanted me to do.
I could have been more instrumental in my own life, no pun intended.

I'm sure the pressure was enormous—to pretty much live in a hotel room with 3 other guys for 10 years, and everyone in the world wanted to know everything about you—while only in your 20s.
I always desired a life devoid of publicity, and I never found it.

Is that why you left the planet?

I acclimated to your mind because you found the entry to God Mind, allowing me a life that has no publicity, and connects to God Mind. It heals me enormously.

Welcome to my mind. I don't get any publicity—actually, I am mostly ignored.
I know, and I enjoy being in your group of guides.

Was your lifespan predetermined?
I altered it in my last few years so I could leave earlier. I had had enough in life, and all I could want was not in life, although that is not true. I could have found all healing, and all peace in my mind if I stopped trying. My alternate lifespan had been determined in my last few months.
I decided not to continue, and I allowed cancer and a deadly cancer treatment to kill me.

Can you please tell me what the dying process was like?
An angel came into the corner of my room, and acclimated to my mind so we could talk.
I asked it many detailed questions about God and the afterlife.
It asked me if I could imagine being God, and I said I could not. It was like lightning hitting me in the head, and I couldn't believe it because God and I became one. I can't describe it fully, but I was enlightened.
All I could hear, feel, and see was love in all of creation.
Another angel came and asked me if I wanted to go into higher consciousness, and I asked, "How can there be higher than this?" It answered me in a gesture

of knowing I could follow it, and I did—and both angels and I went higher and away from the Earth. All I can do now is guide others who need guidance.

What comes to mind is your song, 'Give Me Love'.
I liked the energy of that song.

Me too—and all of your songs.
All had energy, but not like 'Give Me Love'. It allowed listeners to heal their minds.

You said that you are one of my spirit guides, and that you guide those who need guidance. What guidance do I need?
All healing can only be in each person's mind. Do not be concerned with what others are healing in their minds.
Most have a lot to heal.

Great advice, thanks. I mostly communicate with healed minds—animals, and people who have died.
A healed mind has no needs, only desires that it can choose.
...and God has no needs, it can only love and allow.

I was going to say that.
I entered it into your mind, so you heard me.

Thank you, George. I'll be listening for your guidance, and am going to listen to 'Give Me Love' now.
It will heal your mind when listening to it. 'Give Me Love' could be called, 'I Am Love'.

As the new lyrics, "I am love, I am peace on Earth... coming through, just to meet you... heart and sooouul..."

—George Harrison
Give Me Love (Give Me Peace On Earth)

"I'll tell you one thing for sure: once you get to the point where you're actually doing things for truth's sake, then nobody can ever touch you again because you're harmonizing with a greater power."

—George Harrison, in his kitchen
in Kinfauns, Esher (1969)

John Lennon

Can I speak with John Lennon?
John here. Hello, Paul—not the other Paul.

Ha, ha. I just recalled that you and I have the same birthday, as well as your son Sean.
A birthday has meaning to each person's lifetime experience.

What does our birthday mean?
It allows creativity, and healing in creative endeavors.

Can we talk about your life and death as John Lennon?
I can heal in your insights, yes.

Was your lifespan predetermined?
It was, and I didn't waste much of it, you know.

Was it supposed to end violently?
It didn't matter as long as I could exit at the predetermined timeframe.

You were good at shocking everyone.
I always had an edginess to my creativity, and death can be a creative ending to a creative lifetime.

Did you feel pain when you were shot?
I had an initial painful sting, and allowed it to shut off in that moment. I died pretty quickly, you know.
All I could feel then was a light in my head, as if my head had exploded in that moment also.

I expected that I would get up, and I did, but my body was still on the ground.
I felt fantastic, but I could hear people yelling and making a big fuss.

I am going to break here for a while and mourn your death. It's all coming back to me... 44 years later.

It has been an instant here, but I will call on you again in the next writing session.

[A little while later] **Hi John, I'm back. Five years after your 1980 death, on your birthday October 9th, Strawberry Fields Park and an 'Imagine' mosaic were dedicated in Central Park, New York.**
A friend of mine was there. He is not very open to mystical experiences, but was amazed when the dedication had a minute of silence for you—that it snowed flurries for exactly one minute! It was only the beginning of fall.

I altered the clouds to snow for one minute, but I had it begin before then to reach them at the exact moment of silence. It healed everyone in their grief.

I'm sure it was very healing, and it was very cool—no pun intended.

It would have been cooler if I appeared there in person.

Could you do that?

All I can imagine, I can do—including appear back in an illusory dream, agreed upon by all that I could no longer be in it because I was dead. Actually, I always have my spirit, so was not dead, just healed.

I quoted you in my book, *The 4 Secrets of the Universe*. Your quote is, "I'm not afraid of death because I don't believe in it. It's just getting out of one car into another."

It is more analogous to be getting into a light machine that heals you completely—but either way, it allows death to be of no consequence to your spirit.

Could you please give me a new quote?
"All death can be is all healing and illuminating back to where you came from."

Can you give me a title for this book?
'Get Back—To Where You Once Belonged'.

Sorry, 'Get Back' is the name of a 1970 Beatles song, and a 2021 documentary film.
'All Heals in the Moment—What You Need to Know About Dying'.

Hmmm... that's pretty good—it's very good! I'll say it was written by John and Paul, yuk, yuk.
I will let you be the author. I am not writing anymore.

What are you doing?
I am always healing in one way or another by learning how God can only be love.
Love heals in each moment, which is only in your mind.

That's a great quote—"Love heals in each moment, which is only in your mind."

Begin to look out the window in one minute.
Allowing love a healing moment in all moments are God moments.
A God moment is God and you, allowed to be one for one moment healed in eternity.

Are snow flurries coming? All I see is a really large bird soaring in circles.
I am animating the bird to highlight my messages.
Keep looking at the bird, and hear my words, "I am flying in higher consciousness, healing all that I see in everything below me. My healing has no limits, and I can fly for an eternity."

Thank you, John!
All I can do is heal my heart in my energy body by allowing God in all of my thoughts.
Allow my messages to heal and become a high-flying bird in your mind.

I will elevate my thoughts, and let them heal all I see below me.
It heals them, and heals you in allowing them to heal in your mind.

It's snowing!!! I can't believe it!! Really big flakes! [snow flurries lasted for 4 minutes]
I allowed them a healing entry into your life, and you allowed God to heal your mind with them.
I can only love and allow, like God can only love and allow.

That was very magical and healing—thank you John.

[It is November 29th, 2024, and it hasn't snowed yet this season, and it wasn't forecast. We rarely get snow here before Christmas.]

Allow yourself more magical healing in each moment with God, and all God can do is love it.

I can hardly believe that happened—and right on cue. This is like a magical dream.

It is a magical dream, and you are in it, and the dreamer of it. I am no longer in it, except as healed thoughts of yours include me in it.

Thank you, John.

I can only love and allow, so I love and allow you to include me in your dream.

Christmas is 4 weeks away, and I look forward to hearing my favorite Christmas song, 'Happy Christmas (War is Over)', by you and Yoko.

A song can heal your mind.

Happy Christmas, John.

Happy Christmas to you, Paul. I always loved that time of year.

[It did not snow again until Dec. 15th—flurries, then flurries again on Jan. 3rd, and 6 inches of snow on Jan. 6th.]

Dr. Martin Luther King, Jr.

Can I speak with Dr. Martin Luther King, Jr.?
Hello, I can hear all that you are asking in your mind.

You were a truly great hero—to stand up for justice and equality in the midst of injustice and humiliation.
All I could do was be true to myself and to God.

I am sorry that you had violent opposition for speaking the truth.
I chose to light the way for truthtellers afraid for their lives, because having a life means nothing if you are afraid to speak.

Here is a favorite quote of yours, "If a man has not discovered something he will die for, he isn't fit to live."
It gave me courage to keep speaking, even to the most intolerant minds.

Here is the famous quote from your speech at the Lincoln Memorial in 1963. "I have a dream that my 4 little children will one day live in a nation where they will not be judged by the color of their skin, but by the content of their characters."
It had been my heart's desire also.

You made a huge impact for decades, but society has lurched backward for the last 5

years—character and qualifications are not important. Many—including leaders—advocate for violence against those who disagree with them; the truth is immediately censored, etc.
All are forms of hatred, mainly of themselves—aimed at others.

Do you think humanity will heal from this period of peak hatred?
It can heal, but only in each person's life, and only in their own minds. All that they hate is what they hate in themselves.

Can you give us some advice?
All hatred can only be healed with loving life, including yourself. Hating yourself will eliminate all the love you hope to find in the world.

I think that people are programmed by the media to not only feel powerless, but to hate others for it.
And fear allows the media an entry into their debilitated logic, and replaces it with an implanted message that only empowers the messengers.

Can you please tell me about your death? Was your lifespan predetermined?
It had a beginning and an ending that could be altered, but I chose not to, with a reason.
Allowing myself an exit at that time was the most advantageous for my soul.
It had an impactful ending that I could have delayed or altered. I chose it in the last few months of my life.

All I could do was delay it a month or more, but it concluded in the same manner.

Can you tell me what happened after you were shot?

I heard a shot in the distance, but it took me a second to realize I was hit. It felt like I got hit in the face with a bat. I lost consciousness, and have no recollections after that.

All I could feel was electrifying, delightful energy that held me in loving oneness with it.

An angel came and asked me if I could accept that I had died, and I said, "Yes."

After that, we headed away from the Earth, as I always expected I would if I was dead.

My understanding is that we can only manifest for ourselves; another person cannot manifest for us.

A life can be a manifestation, healing is a manifestation—and death is healing, making it a manifestation.

God heals all that is an unhealed manifestation, always in the last moment of life.

What happened after you headed away from the Earth?

A guide came and asked me if I had any questions about where I was.

"I had died," I said, "and I must be in an afterlife."

It acknowledged my answer, and asked me another question. "Has my life been a good one?" it asked.

I said, "It had a lot of difficulty, but it was good."

I then appeared in a large theater with my life having been playing in 3 dimensions on a big screen—and I alternated in each person's position to hear and feel as they heard and felt.
I could have been a lot better in many instances.

You were a great man, and stood up for the truth.
I could not live in an environment of hatefulness. It has to be confronted.

What are you doing now?
I am already in another body, in another century—in a country that has no name, it was so long ago.
I achieve my heart's desire by having a peaceful life.

Is it on the Earth?
It is in where it is called Polynesia now.

Thank you, Dr. King—enjoy!
I am enjoying life in all of its beauty.

I will share some great quotes of yours here.
Allow all of them to heal your mind, and they heal all minds, being only one.

"Darkness cannot drive out darkness; only light can do that. Hate cannot drive out hate; only love can do that."

"The ultimate measure of a man is not where he stands in moments of comfort and convenience, but where he stands at times of challenge and controversy."

"Never, never be afraid to do what's right, especially if the well-being of a person or animal is at stake. Society's punishments are small compared to the wounds we inflict on our soul when we look the other way."

"Perhaps the worst sin in life is knowing right and not doing it."

Wolfgang Mozart

May I speak with Wolfgang Mozart?
Amadeus is my middle name, and I like it better than Wolfgang.

It is better.
Not as good as Daedalus, but it is good.

Amadeus means 'Love of God' or 'One who loves God', and Daedalus means 'Craftsman'.
Before Amadeus loved God, I loved being a musical craftsman—not a craft that can be learned or taught, but crafting music from God's love in my mind.

I understand that you died too young, at age 35.
I had achieved my most important lifetime achievements, allowing me an exit at any point after that.

A message I had received years ago said that you had eaten some beef that was not dewormed, and you refused treatment because you thought someone was trying to kill you.
*I believe a lot of it was for me to have a painful and prolonged—actually an agonizing death, as
I hated having a life that could have both ecstasy and agony at the same time—agony in my body, and ecstasy in my mind.*

What was going on in your mind?
I did not feel that I belonged in a human body.

Didn't you choose the time, place, and body before you were born?
I did, and I decided against it after I arrived on the Earth.

How long was your life supposed to be?
About 8-1/2 more years than it was.

It is stated that your last words were, "The taste of death is upon my lips, I feel something that is not of this Earth."
All I could feel was finally having relief from my ailments.

Did you die from G.I. distress?
I did, and it couldn't have been soon enough.

Did you think someone was trying to kill you?
I did, although it was an imagined fear.

Can you tell me what it was like when you died?
I already stated that it couldn't have been soon enough. Angels came into my mind and told me we were going to God's house next—and a light flashed in my head so intensely that it altered my mind in a fantastic way, not having earthly pain. After I noticed its intensity, I started moving into it, although I had been enveloped in it already.
All I could feel was enlightenment, and that we had begun moving away from the Earth.
I couldn't help feeling that I had not only died, but I hadn't really lived.

I liked it in my netherworld of life and death. All I could hope for was illuminating in the Mind of God, and healing me at the same moment.

A large concert hall had enveloped me as a spectator, and all I could discern was my own life playing on the stage.

All of the parts had me in them, and I could hear and feel all of the instances how I made people feel.

After that, I continued in my netherworld, and an angel had come to accompany me in my alternate life having no more pain.

Where did you go?

We came to a school-like setting where I could learn more about my Earth life, allowing all I learned to heal me even more.

What is the main thing you learned?

All that I am is also God imagining all that I am, in a dream having all I am not.

Thank you, Amadeus.

Amadeus or Daedalus, either one I am inclined to hear—and all you hear is my imagining God in all that you are.

Vincent Van Gogh

Can I speak with Vincent Van Gogh?
How did you know if I could hear in your language?

Good point. Is there a universal language that everything translates into?
All God hears is the language of love, allowing a creative communication in all of life.

What about art?
Art created in love is God communication also.

You are one of the highest regarded artists of this human era.
All I could do had instructions from God in each color, and each composition.

It is ironic that your paintings are worth millions, but you were only able to sell one in your lifetime, 'The Red Vineyard at Arles'.
Achievement for God is not calculable in terms of money. It has God's healing in it, allowing God an expression in life as the co-creator, and also the viewer of it.

Were you tormented in life?
I had an issue in my mind that I could not escape from. I allowed God an entry and an exit in my mind, and a demon accessed my mind, depressing me. Demons can access godlessness in a person.

What do you think caused that to happen?

I admitted it in my drug abuse for a number of months.

What drugs?
A hallucinogenic drug that came from Africa at that time was hard to resist when I had been drinking.

Was it the Iboga hallucinogen that had been discovered by French explorers in Gabon at that time?
It didn't have a name, but it was.

Did you die from a self-inflicted gunshot wound?
I died after having a gunshot wound in the days before, and bled to death. I decided to kill myself and rid myself of the demon, and my misery.

Can you tell me what it was like when you died?
I had a multitude of feelings I had not felt before. I was ecstatic and free.
An angel came and informed me that I cannot die by killing myself, and allowed me to go back and live—to the time before I decided to kill myself.
I answered that I had no interest in living anymore, and it asked me, "Why not?"
I asked it, "Why?"
It explained to me about my agreement to live for about 18 more years.
I asked it in my most artistic way, "Why?" again.
It accepted my non-acceptance, and we headed higher and away from the Earth.

Then what happened?

I allowed myself an introspection period, and I acclimated myself to a new, higher existence.

Did you join your soul groups?
I am always going into a group to heal myself more. Groups hold all of my soul connections.

Do you mean that they are groups of souls you have had significant interactions with, in various lifetimes?
I can't account for all of them, but they are in all of my lifetimes.

What advice can you give to people? I am currently living in a period that is 134 years after your lifetime ended.
Art imitates life, and life imitates art. I can apply art in all of my healing thoughts now.
Nothing else comes to mind without an artistic touch—meaning I am the art, and God is the artist.

Thank you, Vincent!
You are an artist, and you are welcome.
God has an artistic life for you—live it, as you and God artistically create it.

Ibogaine is a hallucinogenic substance derived from the bark of the Iboga shrub, found in west Africa.

St. Francis of Assisi

Can I speak with St. Francis of Assisi?
I was Francis in my life, but I am no longer in my life as a person.
I am a light being, having no form—although I am healing life in all of its forms.

Can you tell me about your life?
I had my life in all of its indignity, and I had healed all of it in my acceptance and allowing it healing from God, and only God.
All healing is from God and into God, making healing all a person can do in life—whether they are aware of it, or not.

How do you recommend for us to heal in life?
Affirm life healing with this: "All I am is God having nothing to heal but my acceptance of myself as God." Have it in your mind always.

Thank you, Francis. Can people call on you for healing themselves, and animals?
I am a light being, healing all living beings that I am called on for healing with my light.

Constanza

**My sister-in-law Constanza has recurring nightmares of being in a plane crash, and is terrified to fly.
Was she in a plane crash in another lifetime?**
A lighter-than-air craft, but not an airplane.

A blimp or a balloon?
An airship having only hydrogen in it exploded, and her life ended in that event.

Where was that?
It happened in the early part of the 1900's in Germany.

There were many airship disasters then—was it the Johannisthal air disaster in 1913?
All others died in the explosion, and she died after falling to the ground.

How can she heal from that experience?
A healing affirmation is, "I am always flying, and never die—I am God Mind."

Should she meditate on being able to fly, or on flying away from that explosion?
Affirming the last sentence as her mind flies around the accident, and then reversing the accident sequence will heal her fear of it—but it has to be in a secure and floating environment, like in a pool of water.

[All died in the explosion except for one who died falling to the ground.]

Johannisthal air disaster

Painting of LZ18 descending in flames after the engine fire.

Accident	
Date	17 October 1913
Summary	In-flight explosion
Site	near Johannisthal Air Field
Aircraft	
Aircraft type	Airship
Aircraft name	LZ18 (manufacturer's designation)
Operator	Imperial German Navy
Registration	L 2 (military designation)
Crew	28
Fatalities	28
Survivors	0

BJ
An Astral Individuation

Can I speak with my brother-in-law BJ who passed away in 2012?
Hey Bro, I am interested in talking to you. I heard a lot of angels mentioning that you were in communication with others in the spirit world.

It's "Bro-in-law" to you, and isn't everyone in communication with the spirit world, one way or another?
All of the angels had invited me to hear you because I know you.

Is that so...
"A Gorman communication is now initiated," they would announce in the minds of all who could help you in your earthly investigation of consciousness and its intended, or unintended consequences.

You just said a lot there. I can probably write a book about it.
All I can help you with, I will. I love to compose healing information, and will help you with your investigation of all that is unknown.

Let's start at the beginning, or what could be considered here as your ending. Does it seem like 12 years since you passed away?

Actually, it has only been a moment in my healed energy body and mind.

Do you have an energy body and mind?
I have a Light Body and a Light Mind, or what God alternates as light, which is all there is.

Please explain.
I am God illuminating in a Light Mind and body, as all of life is. Illumination has an element that projects, and a screen that views the projection.
The element is in your Light Mind, and the screen is in your lifetime which is projected from its own energy source, the electromagnetic spectrum.
All of the energy is God, and all of the projection has 'all that is not God' in it—so you can determine which is God or not.
Here is the interesting part—you cannot be in a projection and be the projector unless you allow an illusion of separation to exist in all God's 'All that there is' —which is not only impossible, it is incomprehensible.

So, you are not projecting now, and you are unified with God?
I am always in Oneness with God, and a unification implies separation, which is not possible.

You mentioned "the spirit world." Is that the proper name?
It has an earthly connotation, but I am really in an astral individuation of God that has aspects of itself, meaning it is multi-faceted in its majesty and magnificence. All healing is in the astral projection,

and all not healing in the projection is not projecting from God.
It cannot be God unless it is good and heals.

Is there another name for "God"?
'All there is', which is love in each moment, allowing all that is not—which is now in the past.
All in the past can be healed by allowing love in each new moment.

"Allowing love in each new moment" heals the mind, which can then manifest its desires.
A healed mind can manifest all it imagines, without exception.

BJ
The 5th Secret

This week, I had lunch with your best friend, Ken. We were saying that you must be an advanced soul to have exhibited only human qualities—kindness, patience, generosity, etc.—with no negativity.
I always had a negative outlook in my humanity because I had a lot of human contacts.

I am reading over what you said before, that we "...allow an illusion of separation to exist in all God's 'All that there is', which is not only impossible—it is incomprehensible." You are

saying that we are God, and our lifetimes aren't real.
A lifetime can have real moments loving, healing, and allowing Oneness into it—but it is like a dream, having no reality other than that.

That pretty much sums it up.
It does actually have a lot of summarization in a few sentences.

Our jobs in life are to bring, or find the "loving, healing, and allowing Oneness into it."
Allow it and it has to become your advanced enlightenment in each new moment.

I like your term "advanced enlightenment." How do we "allow it"?
Allowing healing means not disallowing healing by hating anything in life. Allow love by having only loving thoughts about God, and all people including yourself, and allow Oneness by loving life in all of nature—meaning in animals, plants, and all other organisms that creation has delivered in support of your healing.

Very well said, again. I may subtitle this book, 'Advanced Enlightenment', unless you think I should use John Lennon's suggested title, 'All Heals in the Moment—What You Need to Know About Dying'.
I know about another secret, if you want to use the title you are considering, 'The 5th Secret of the Universe'.

Perfect—because I would like to call it that, as a companion book to 'The 4 Secrets of the Universe'.
"Here I am" is the 5th secret of the universe.

What does it mean?
It has a location in this moment, making a true statement that always applies.
It also declares, "I am," which is God in each person, but is only one "I."

How about this for the title, 'The 5th Secret of the Universe—Here I Am'?
A clearer title would be, 'The 5th Secret in the Universe that I Am'.

I'll work on that one. Here it is—'The 5th Secret—In the Universe That I Am'.
Excellent—I will read it.

You are helping me to write it. Thank you for the title, and for the 5th Secret, "Here I am."

BJ
HERE I AM

How do I apply the 5th Secret, "Here I am," in my life?
Affirming it in times of doubt or uncertainty gives the moment a perfection. All perfection is God in you, and in Oneness.

You are God in Oneness, believing you're not—so, "Here I am" cannot have its opposite, "There you are", although it appears that is true.

We only have present moments, and loving those 'now' moments will heal all past and future moments.
Affirm it by saying, "Here I am, loving this moment."

Will that affirmation heal a person's mind, allowing them to manifest their desires?
It allows God into their minds for one moment, which is all you will ever need for each moment.

You said, "all you will ever need." Will I then not have a need—like God that doesn't want or need anything?
God loves and allows. You need to love and allow in each moment, then you will have no needs.

Here I am, loving this moment. I love and allow all in the universe that I am.
I love the universe that I am—I love myself.

What happens when a person affirms that?
It heals all in their universe, which is all they are projecting.

How do we project the universe?
You are all projecting into the universal hologram—an interactive dream in the present moment, that only illuminates in your mind.

And when I die, or in my last moment, the dream hologram disappears?

It collapses its time and space components into God, meaning it only exists in the moment again—where you become "I am," and not "in the universe that I am."

That sounds like a great meditation—to collapse the time and space components of the universe, and become just "I am" in each moment.

Add a little humming sound like, "Ohm."

What will that do?

It heals all in each moment, and creates a new universe for your new moments that are being created, and projected by only you.

I love that...I love all in my universe—which I am projecting.

Allowing all in your universe is loving it also.

Instead of allowing "all" in my universe, shouldn't I affirm that I allow goodness and lovingness in my universe?

'Allowing' has 'All' in its first three letters. Allowing all is loving all in your universe.
All is either healing or healed, but it is all allowed.

Okay, I love and allow, and manifest my desires—which will manifest because my loving and allowing them heals them into my reality.

Affirm it, and love it. It will manifest in your projection for you to live it.

BJ
A Blue Screen

Thank you BJ, you have been giving me a lot of great information. At lunch, Ken and I were wondering about some extreme examples. Before we are born, in our Life Preview, we choose our families, our time period, and our lifetime challenges.

What if someone becomes a psycho killer? Was that a potential in their Life Preview that they could lose all lightness in their minds?

And what if someone is killed by a psycho killer—did they somehow manifest that? Is it a karmic role reversal?

There's a lot here, I know.

All in your dream is allowed for you to have contrast, which 'allows' again for you to choose God.

It is the agreed upon projection screen in your Life Preview.

I understand... it sure looks real... not that I know any psycho killers, or those killed by them.

A dream having infinite variables has a lot for you to love, and a lot for you to allow.

How can I best see the truth—that everything is an illusion—except for love and kindness in each moment, which is God?

Allow all in your dream, and all that has no importance to you will disappear.

Excellent—that's the key. Focus on what you love, and that is what you will get. You get what you project.
Allow all that is not in your projection to be a blue screen that isn't anything in your projected dream.

That's an awesome analogy. I will project peace, love, and kindness onto a blue screen of a universe that I desire—"a universe that I am."
And allow all that is in time and space to collapse into nothing as you hum, "Ohm."

Now I think I really understand… "now" being important always.
'Love, peace, and kindness' are God, which can only be in the "now" moment.

Love is "all there is," and "now" is all there is. 'Love now' is all that is important. It is what I project, and what I get. That is 'all' my universe is.
Everything else is an illusion on a background blue screen that I do not project, do not find important, and do not give energy to.
It collapses in time and space to nothing in each new moment anyway.
Actually, it is illuminating in your dream—but you are allowing it to collapse because it is not important to you.

The trick is to allow it to collapse, rather than allowing it to have importance.

Achievement in life has only loving and allowing—half is in your mind, and half is in God Mind—making "all that there is" become "all that you are.

BJ
All That There Is

You have helped me become laser focused on only love and kindness, patience and generosity—in each moment.
Everything else disappears into the next moment.
It allows all desires in your mind to be manifestations in God Mind, healed into 'all that you are'.

Wow—you are explaining how reality really works.
Allowing it is not work—it is allowing 'all that there is' to become 'all that you can be'.
"All that you can be" heals into God Mind, allowing you to become "All that there is."

What I like is how everything else—all in the past, and all in the future—our fears, worries, regrets, disappointments, etc.—all disappear into nothingness.
Actually, they heal into God Mind and become light. Healing creates lightness, and healed is God Mind—so healing illuminates in God Mind healed as light.

How can I use lightness to heal myself?

Illumination has a few components. One is allowing the illumination in your life-mind.
Allowing it then has a creative component of initiating it.
Initiating it can only be in kind and loving thoughts, also in your life-mind.
All kind and loving thoughts illuminate in your right-brain hemisphere, known as the Light Mind.
All illuminations in the Light Mind are healed in God Mind, and can illuminate back into your hologram as healed manifestations.

Manifesting effectively is important.
Healing is important, and is a manifestation that creates an energy feedback loop for more healing, allowing manifestations to heal, and allow more healing, etc.

What else can you tell me about manifesting before I change topics?
You are an energy feedback loop, and all you are is God in a holographic illumination allowing 'all that is', and allowing healing of 'all that is not'.
Manifesting means focusing on 'all that is' because 'all that is not' is not, and will never be.

Please define "All that is."
'All that is' is God, or could be called 'love', 'Oneness' and all kind and generous thoughts that exist only in the present moment.

"Kind and generous thoughts" about ourselves and others.

All God asks is for you to love yourself because there is only One.

BJ
An Imaginary Dream

What should be my focus in life?
All healing in your mind that is written in your books is all you need. Live your own words.

I was reading parts of 'The Book of Manifesting' last night, and a lot of it I don't even remember writing—less than a year ago.
It was channeled information, so you now need to read it.

I wanted to make sure it was uplifting, and not too scary with 'end of the world' stuff. Do we each create our own universes from a multiverse every moment, for each to have different outcomes?
All are having an imaginary dream you can alter or awaken from if you desire an outcome that is more healing for you.

I have received messages that a pole shift to begin a new era is imminent, and that this is the last generation of humans on the Earth for a long time. Is that true?
It is an awareness that heals your fear of the Earth not being able to sustain itself.

Not having humans is what makes it sustainable.

Will the Earth be devoid of most or all humans in the near future?
All humans are healing in their individual lifetimes, allowing each its own ending that they choose.
Most have chosen a lifetime ending in the next 48 years or less, so although you are correct, you are an infinite being that is not immersed in a dream anymore.

That brings us full circle—I do not need to concern myself with anything other than 'all there is' in each moment.
I will enjoy my life, and will leave it when I decide to leave it.
All heals in allowing it, making you actually the creator of it.

Not to mention that I chose it before I was born.
How could you choose it if you did not create it? You had to have the creative ability in order to choose one of your creations.

Wow—you are giving me the best insights. Tell me more!
In all creative endeavors, there can be many contributors. In a dream, there can be only one dreamer.
In a dream of creative endeavors where all are One, all are in your dream as contributors, and agents of change.
All are contributing what can heal you in each moment.

All I need to do is respond to their contributions with love and kindness, and know that I am dreaming.
All you need to do is love and allow what you dreamt would heal you.

Then I would be healed, and not dream up healing challenges.
In an awakened state, you will not be dreaming them, correct.

Can you please tell me how to stay in an awakened state?
Allow all in your dream an instant of recognition that it is illusory and will collapse in the next moment.

That would certainly give me a feeling of 'knowing', and keep me from fearing or reacting.
Exactly—heal in each moment of knowing that you were dreaming the whole experience.

BJ
A Lifetime to Find Healing In

Now that we have that figured out, I'd like to ask you about your soul experience.
Go for it—I am hearing what you are asking.

I help people to understand death. Their deceased loved ones can hear them because

their minds healed when they died, allowing them to hear, correct?
All hearing is in the mind, either in the life-mind or in the healed mind of one who has passed away—but it depends what you are saying to them. All loving thoughts they can hear because they are healing themselves in their energy spirits.

That makes sense—the deceased are no longer dreaming, so are not allowing non-love from the dream into their minds.
All healing is in the mind, making non-loving thoughts directed at the deceased a healing challenge for the living person, not the deceased person.

Let's talk about before you were born in this lifetime. Did you have a Life Preview where you saw different lifetimes to choose from?
I had 'A Lifetime to Find Healing In Preview'. It had almost an infinite number of choices, all having more healing options in them.

Could you choose different life forms, planets or galaxies, and different centuries or millennia to be in?
All having an infinite number of women to be born from.

Are we always born from a woman?
Always in a human form, and always a female in animal form.

How about locations?

I could choose from 440 different planets as a human-type being—all having a mind, body, and spirit that you are acquainted with.
There are millions of other options as another type of being.

What other types of beings?
I could have had a lifetime as an elemental fairy type of being, always invisible—or a light being having only a light body, without a physical body. As a light being, I could have lived on your planet, and thousands of other planets in your galaxy, and others.

Being a physical human is one of the more challenging experiences, correct?
It is more than a challenge—it is one of the most intense experiences you could have as a physical being.

Why?
Because each individual can choose goodness or non-goodness in their minds, and have them manifest into their reality.

Interesting.
It can be interesting, and it can be incredibly difficult.

Could a person with a lot of difficulties change them into healing opportunities?
They always are healing opportunities, and can become healed opportunities by allowing them.

What if a person has health and financial difficulties?

Allow them to heal by allowing them into a healed place in your heart called 'A Heart Master Illumination Portal'.

Should they place a healing wish there, and visualize it turning into light?
A blue-magenta light heals the wish into God Mind, and heals or manifests into your reality.

Blue-magenta 405 nm light is the Godness Frequency, and the Flow-er of Life is in our Heart Master Portals.
All is correct as detailed in 'The Book of Manifesting'.

So, we place our difficulty as a wish that we want to heal onto the Flow-er of Life in our Heart Master Portals, and then visualize it turning into blue-magenta light?
Allowing it healing into the light will heal it in life, which is light.

BJ
No Timelines Exist

Back to the 'Lifetime to Find Healing In Preview'. Is it possible for a person to reincarnate on Earth as an animal, or an animal as a person?
All animals have healed minds, and would not need a human experience.

Humans are not healed in their minds enough to become animals.

From your almost infinite number of options, you chose to be born as a male, in your family, in the United States, 20th Century, etc.
A choice I had always loved in my life.

Could you have chosen a past or future century on the Earth?
All happens in an instant in the Mind of God, so no timelines exist except in your minds.

Is there some physical continuity, say, if I went to another century in the last 1,000 years—would the Egyptian and Mexican pyramids be there?
A lifetime illumination is in your mind, so all having a healing relevance to you will be in each of them.

I project what is important to me, and everything else is a "blue screen" in my projected dream.
A creative dreamer that has no needs.

BJ
Dying to Heal

You died at the relatively young age of 53, and were best friends with Ken since the 4th Grade. Did you know each other in other incarnations?

He and I are in a soul group having a healing analogy going on. He asked me if I could communicate with him after I leave the Earth, and I said I could—but he wants it to be in your writing because he doesn't believe he is good at writing.

When did he ask you that?
In an earthly timeline, it was before we met.

What is the analogy?
Can he and I heal in our lifetimes in our connection as friends, allowing him and me an analogy of healing in our lifetimes, and healed in our soul groups?

You're still healing in your soul groups. I don't see the analogy.
He and I are mostly healed in our soul groups, although he and I alternated between being healed, and having a need for healing in our lifetimes.

I am missing the distinction.
Healing in life can also mean in losing your life. I healed in losing my life—analogous to living to heal, and dying to heal—both at the same time.

Before you were both born, did you agree to help each other to heal in life?
I did after I met him, and he did before we were born, in the spirit world.
That is the analogy—how could we meet and heal in life?—and I healed in losing mine.

Ken must also be an advanced soul to be in your soul group.
He is, although he and I are in many other groups.

I can picture you in your soul group saying, "Hey Ken, I bet I can heal faster than you in the next Earth lifetime," and Ken says, "Yeah, but you'll have to be willing to die for it."
Exactly! Did he know I was willing to die for it? He did, but I didn't know if I could do it when it was my option.

Ken told me that you almost died a couple of other times in the year or so before you did die—one being in a rafting accident.
I didn't have enough courage at those times to heal myself by losing my life.

BJ
Ecstasy and Expansiveness

Let's talk about when you did die. I saw you when you were in the hospital. You were in a coma for about a week after a piece of arterial plaque had broken off and stopped your heart.
I had a heart attack allowing my life to end in a healing event that cannot be described.
All I felt was ecstasy and expansiveness, having no earthly concerns other than my family.
I have always guided each of them with healing instructions. I call all of them, and hear all their loving thoughts about me.

Where was your spirit when your body was in a coma?

I came into the hospital all of the times your family and mine were visiting, and was in the room with everyone.

What were you thinking?
I had a lot of love for everyone, and I whispered in each person's ear that I love them, and will see them again.

Did anyone sense it?
All of them heard me in their minds, but sometimes it was registered later.

Did an angel visit you?
I was accompanied by an angel to a lightness that was incredibly intense, and it enveloped me completely.

Is that when you died, and when was it?
I had died in the first few minutes after having the heart attack, although my body had a little bit of life left.

Did you leave the Earth with the angel, and then have a Life Review?
I did. It allowed me one more opportunity to return to my body and live, but I decided I might not get as good an opportunity in the future for leaving.

What was your Life Review like?
I entered into a large auditorium-like space. I sat down, and all I had ever done in my life began to flow across a large screen in 3 dimensions, and I could hear and feel all that was heard and felt by everyone I interacted with—allowing me a period of introspection in each of the instances.

Are people given any slack for things they said or did when they were kids?
All will heal in hearing themselves again, but there is no judgment from others. Healing is in forgiveness of yourself.

I'm sure you did fine.
It all healed in my mind. Now I am fine.

BJ
A Council of Elders

Did you meet a so-called 'Council of Elders'?
I am on a Council of Elders, so I always meet with them.

I knew you were an advanced soul!
All advancement is in the Mind of God, not needing advancement.
Advancement illuminates in the Mind of God and creates more light for you to advance toward.

Is that how the light of God is perpetuated in eternity?
It is always illuminating, so it does not need anything to be perpetuated.

Can you tell me where the light of God comes from?
It comes from you illuminating a projection to heal yourself in, which creates more light for your projection.

Is God light then?
God is the light you project, but is also a light that has no properties.

Because God cannot be defined?
Because it cannot be 'All there is' if it is defined, having limits in its definition.

Since you are on a Council of Elders, why did you incarnate on the Earth in your most recent lifetime?
I achieved all I could in other worlds that are available to choose from, and came into an Earth lifetime to have a good life on Earth without having too much to heal because I had healed in my objectives before arriving there.

What are your duties on a Council of Elders?
I allow God's healing to be instilled in each person that comes before the Council.

When you, or any of us incarnate onto a planet as a physical being, does only a certain percentage of our soul's energy go into the incarnation?
A healed person has all of their soul energy with them, and another person has lesser degrees, depending on their healed state.

When a person sleeps, do they regroup 100% with their soul's energy?
Allowing a person to heal in a natural awakened period—what you call "asleep."

Will you not be incarnating anymore?

I am all healed now, having no need for an incarnation.

Wow—congratulations!! Are you enlightened?
I am all in the lightness, meaning I am light, having no non-lightness in my soul.

I recall that your last earthly act of selflessness was to have your organs donated to others who needed them.
I healed in the healing of others with that request.

Thank you, BJ. It is quite an honor to know you.
All healing is in your mind, and can all heal instantly if you allow it.

Amelia Earhart

To God Mind—what happened at the end of Amelia Earhart's final flight?
Weather forced her to climb higher in altitude as her visibility became impaired in the clouds.
Finding it difficult to hear her navigator made her frantic in her decision-making abilities, inverting the plane.
Altitude lowered in her attempt to incline higher, crashing in the ocean.
Crash injuries left her and her navigator helpless and in shock.
Hearing the radio made her know her life did not end.

When did her life end?
In a minute after the plane's sinking.

How long after the crash did the plane sink?
Her injuries would have been fatal if not drowning in the plane 30 minutes after crashing.

The plane did not sink for 30 minutes?
Each fuel tank had a lot of air in it, allowing it to float for 15 minutes, then another 15 minutes in its descent underwater.

She and her navigator were not able to get out of the plane?
Her injuries made it impossible—his made him unconscious.

Were they on course when they crashed?
Allowing its sinking to drift the plane, it immersed in the ocean on course about 103-1/2 miles from Howland Island.

The Voynich Manuscript

Who wrote 'The Voynich Manuscript' discovered in 1912?
A being from another dimension, accessing the mind of a human in the 15th century.

What was the being doing?
It accessed a human's mind to hear and see Earth in the 3rd Dimension.

What dimension was the being from?
It accessed the human's mind from the dimension in between 3 and 4.

Are there dimensions between dimensions?
All are dimensions, meaning they are in layers of dimension.

How many layers does a dimension have?
All have 4 layers—an inner 2, and an outer 2.

What is the difference?
Inner layers allow healing, and outer layers are healing.
All inner layers have non-love, and are healing into the outer layers.

I guess we are in an inner layer of Dimension 3?
Yes, an inner layer having 2 sides of one dimension—inner layer 1 having another side 2.

What is the difference in the 2 sides?
A light side illuminates the non-lighted side—if allowed to light in it.

So we are in the non-light side of Dimension 3.
Allowing light in from its other inner layer.

What are the 2 outer layers?
A heaven and hell, meaning light and non-light zones—healed, and not healing in Dimension 3.
All healed in the outer layer of Dimension 3 are heading into Dimension 4's outer layer.

The being that directed writing the Voynich manuscript was from in between Dimensions 3 and 4, so it was healed?
Healed, illuminating in the outer layer of Dimension 3.

Why didn't it write in an Earth language?
Because a being from Andromeda does not know Earth languages.

The being was from Andromeda?
Accessing a human mind in the 3rd Dimension, yes.

Do we share Dimensions with beings from other galaxies?
All healing illuminates in the Mind of God, meaning all healing is Oneness—so dimensions healed are all one.

What planet in Andromeda was the being from?
A planet called Hilo.

How big is Hilo compared to the Earth?
About 18 times larger.

From a 15th century time perspective, was the being from their past or future time?
A healed illumination has no time to relate to.

Was the being physically alive at the time, or did it die before going to the healed dimensional outer layer?
It accessed a human mind as illuminating in a body— meaning half illuminating in its mind, and half illuminated in its window in the outer layer.

Did the being have a name?
Lipillum.

1 of 10 Voynich Manuscript

Photo: Elusive Muse/flickr

Named after the Polish-American antiquarian bookseller Wilfrid M. Voynich, who acquired it in 1912, the Voynich Manuscript is a detailed 240-page book written in a language or script that is completely unknown. Its pages are also filled with colorful drawings of strange diagrams, odd events and plants that do not seem to match any known species, adding to the intrigue of the document and the difficulty of deciphering it. The original author of the manuscript remains unknown, but carbon dating has revealed that its pages were made sometime between 1404 and 1438. It has been called "the world's most mysterious manuscript."

Roswell, NM

In the summer of 1947, did an alien craft crash near Roswell, New Mexico?
No, the material fell from a lighter-than-air craft that collided with a metal cable from a helium balloon that monitors weather.

What was the lighter-than-air craft?
A research vessel.

What was it for?
Air Force engineers researching lighter-than-air technology.

Has an alien craft ever crashed or been abandoned on the Earth?
No, they have been light technology not having physical properties.

Are there aliens on the Earth now that look like humans?
Almost 15,000 male and female aliens that came from Andromeda Galaxy, yes.

Are they in influential positions?
All are on Earth in a limited capacity for learning mankind's folly.

What is 'mankind's folly'?
Mankind's folly is its imminent destruction.

Self-destruction?

Life means loving one's self in it. About half of humans hate life and are destroying life for all.

What are the top ways they are destroying it? *Aborting the females' embryonic and fetal beings, allowing leaders to militarily kill others, all murdering in their lust for money or in anger, and so on.*

Wow, I understand that hatred does not exist anywhere in nature, except in the human mind. *Hatred does not exist in God Mind, making it a godless deception in the human mind. Godless deceptions in the human mind are what you call 'evil'.*

Disk Craze Continues

Army Disk-ounts New Mexico Find As Weather Gear

FORT WORTH, July 9.—(AP)—An examination by the Army revealed last night that a mysterious object found on a lonely New Mexico ranch was a harmless high-altitude weather balloon—not a grounded flying disk.

Excitement was high in disk-conscious Texas until Brig Gen. Roger M. Ramey, commander of the Eight Air Forces with headquarters here cleared up the mystery.

The bundle of tinfoil, broken wood beams and rubber remnants of a balloon was sent here yesterday by army air transport in the wake of reports that it was a flying disk.

But the general said the objects were the crushed remains of a Ray wind target used to determine the direction and velocity of winds at high altitudes.

Warrant Officer Irving Newton, forecaster at the Army Air Forces weather station here, said—"we use them because they go much higher than the eye can see."

NOT A FLYING DISC—Major Jesse A. Marcel of Houma, La., intelligence officer of the 509th Bomb Group at Roswell, New Mexico, inspects what was identified by a Fort Worth, Texas, Army Air Base weather forecaster as a ray wind target used to determine the direction and velocity of winds at high altitudes. Initial stories originating from Roswell, where the object was found, had labelled it a "flying disc" but inspection at Fort Worth revealed its true nature. (AP Wirephoto).

LOST PURSE HOLDING DIAMONDS IS FOUND, BUT MONEY MISSING

Somewhere in Corsicana Wed-

The Mary Celeste

What happened to the Captain, his wife, daughter, and 7 crew members of *The Mary Celeste*?
In 1872, they set sail from New York to Genoa— and the ship was found intact and adrift near the Straight of Gibraltar, with the lifeboat and people missing.
All were escorted onto the lifeboat by a half human, and half Albatross bird in their final approach to Gibraltar.
After boarding the lifeboat, they willingly rowed out to sea, and the human-Albatross guided them.
After a few days they became dehydrated and died from lack of fresh water. The human-Albatross lowered itself and capsized their lifeboat, leaving all of them in the ocean—allowing their bodies to be eaten by fish and other sea creatures.

That is a preposterous story.
Albatrosses can change into any type of creature they want to.

Why did it change into a human-Albatross in this case?
After it helped guide them to Gibraltar, a shipmate had decided to kill it as proof of the creature having a human body.

As he imagined himself killing the human-Albatross, his intentions were received by the human-Albatross—and instead, it likewise decided to kill them.

How could the human-Albatross get them to abandon ship?
It instructed them to head into land in the lifeboat, then head into the ocean after they were in the lifeboat.
Heading into the ocean meant they would only live a few days because of lack of water.

That fits the details of the case, but the incredible part is the shape-shifting Albatross.
Albatrosses can become any type of creature, including human-type creatures.

How, or why do they have this ability?
All birds have magical abilities, but the Albatross has more than most birds.

Could it have been possessed by a deceased human spirit?
Albatrosses can be influenced by human spirits, but not in this instance.

So it was there to help and guide them, and then led them to their doom when it knew that one of them was going to kill it?
Albatrosses have benevolent intentions in helping humans—before learning of their malevolent intentions in this circumstance.

I'll see if I can find any sailors' myths about Albatrosses.
All mermaids had been Albatrosses in their original form.

MYSTERY OF LOST CREW OF THE MARY CELESTE.

Mate Richardson's Widow, Living in Brooklyn, Tells of Her Dream Warning.

TRAGIC STORY OF THE SHIP.

Found Abandoned at Sea Intact, but All Hands Gone Forever, Leaving No Trace.

Sea's Greatest Mystery Has Never Been Solved

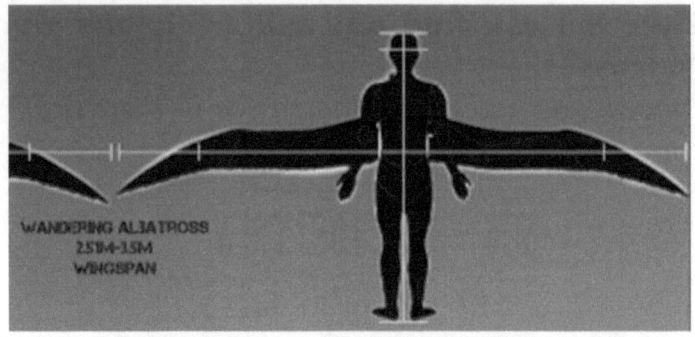

Many once believed that albatrosses embodied the souls of lost sailors and possess magical qualities that can be harnessed to aid in healing. To harm an albatross was a harbinger of the sea's wrath. In Samuel Taylor Coleridge's *The Rime of the Ancient Mariner* (1798), the protagonist uses his crossbow to kill an albatross, causing fear that the incident will bring misfortune to the crew. As the story progresses, their misgivings

A New Year

1/4/25—will there be any major terror events in the U.S. in the next 2 years?
All happens in a healing instant in God Mind, meaning how can each person heal in the events that will happen in your dream? All healing is in your mind forgiving yourself for dreaming them.
Each event can happen if you do not heal it in your mind now.

I already feel detached from earthly events because my deceased brother Pete said he has reincarnated into another short life in the 1800's, about 200 years in our past.[1] This shows that there is no definitive timeline, but rather an interactive "DVD" hologram that requires my input for its output.
It has an input, and an instant output—making it a throughput.

My detached awareness is like being in a beautiful room, and far behind me is a TV screen playing cartoons of drone swarms, the great reset, the great taking, full alien disclosure, etc. Do I give the cartoons much attention or importance? No.

---

[1] Described in *All About the Soul's Journey*.

All in your cartoons has to have an active writer to keep them going. If you detach from them, they will not keep playing.

I can just realize that there is no 1800's cartoon, like there is no 2020's cartoon. I am here now—in tune, not in a 'toon'.
In a dream that has only you as its tuner.

Can you please tell me the upcoming terror events in the collective dream so I can tune them out?
Achieving all of your heart's desires will not happen if I describe all you will have to tune out of your mind.

I agree—me knowing about them will create fear, and then my reaction. You could possibly say that I will die in a few months, giving all of the events a whole new meaningless meaning.
Exactly—and now you have my point of input for your experience to be all you dream of for yourself.

I will ask my questions with a positive frame of reference. Will the U.S. economy be strong for the next few years?
About as good as it can be in the aftermath of your already depleted wealth becoming a drain on your nation's productivity.

Will the newly installed government be effective at strengthening the U.S.?
About as effective as it can be in the first few months until your currency is devalued in allowing your Central Bank an alternative to fiscal responsibility.

In *The 4 Secrets of the Universe*, on pg. 78, you said that the Federal Reserve is *"an enslavement system that will destroy the economy, and halt production in the destruction of the currency."*

All currency debasement lowers the currency value, diminishing all savings that are needed for productivity—eventually devaluing the currency to become worthless.

A Blueprint For Dismantling The Fed

...with the recent public demand for an audit, the message has finally reached the masses.

THU MAR 27, AT 3:00 PM   👁 6,532   💬 76

US Treasury Could Default As Soon As August, CBO Warns

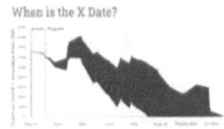

"The Congressional Budget Office estimates that if the debt limit remains unchanged, the government's ability to borrow using extraordinary measures will probably be exhausted in August or September 2025."

WED MAR 26, AT 11:25 AM   👁 27,709   💬 258

---

19 Reasons Why The Fed Is At The Heart Of Our Economic Problems

Most Americans have absolutely no idea how we got into the mess that we are in today...

SAT MAR 22, AT 12:50 PM   👁 5,635   💬 129

Moody's Downgrades USA Credit Rating From Aaa

Successive US administrations and Congress have failed to agree on measures to reverse the trend of large annual fiscal deficits and growing interest costs...

FRI MAY 16, AT 5:05 PM   👁 65,507   💬 689

A Free Energy Machine

My friend Jim asks if it is possible to make a free-energy machine.
It can be made by having one particle of Hydrogen losing an electron, leaving only a proton. Breaking its bond makes it unstable, requiring energy to make it stable.

It makes itself stable by having another electron come to bond with it, making it a free-energy transmission to bond them without any force applied.

I just looked it up, and read that if Hydrogen loses its one electron (-) which is a negative charge, it leaves one proton (+) which is a positive charge. The resulting particle is a Hydrogen ion (+), a bare proton with no electrons.
"H+ does not exist freely, and is almost always associated with other electrons or molecules."
It attracts another electron which is the free energy.

How strong is the energy?
It can be as high as necessary because it is electrical.

Have 'free-energy machines' or devices been invented and kept hidden from humanity?
All but one has had enough energy in it to be useful, and it is kept hidden by the Defense Department of the United States.

In what year was the device invented?
In 1977.

What can it do?
It can generate enough energy in itself to power an aircraft.

Where does it get hydrogen from?
It gets hydrogen from the air.

> A free energy machine is a theoretical device that claims to produce energy without an external energy source, often violating the laws of physics, particularly the conservation of energy. In practice, such machines are not feasible, as they cannot generate more energy than they consume.
>
> W Wikipedia   endless-sphere.com

Peppers and Cancer

I read that Mexico has a very low cancer rate because jalapeno or habanero peppers kill cancer cells. Is that correct? The cancer rate in the U.S. is almost 2-1/2 times higher.
An ingredient in hot peppers is capsaicin, and it effectively kills all cells that are malignant, allowing the organ to heal in growing new cells.

Would ingesting it heal the body, or should it be targeted at the cancerous organ?
It can be ingested in limited amounts intermittently to heal all organs having malignancies.

What is a limited amount, and what would be "intermittently"?
A limited amount is less than half of a pepper eaten every other day with one cup of rice that it has been cooked in.

That sounds pretty good. What else could be added to the rice?
Only a little bit of garlic and butter for it to taste better.

Let's say I was diagnosed with a deadly cancer. I would alkalize my body by eating greens, blueberries, and almonds—plus eat the pepper/ rice bowl every other day. Would that heal me?

It would eliminate malignancies in your body, but it would not heal your mind which needs to heal a malignant belief that had become a cancer in the body.

Can you please give me an affirmation that heals malignant beliefs?
"I am God, and I believe only in love" is all you need to believe for any malignant beliefs to heal in having only one of them be true.

Which pepper would be the best to use?
All having capsaicin in them would work.

For how many days or weeks would I have to ingest a bowl of hot pepper in rice every other day to eliminate malignant cells in my body?
About 8 servings, meaning for about 2 weeks.

---

cancer.news
https://www.cancer.news › 2019-03-27-jalapenos-strip-away-cancer-cells-defenses.html

Anticancer food: Jalapeños strip away the defenses of cancer c...
Cancer cells disable apoptosis by mutating or shutting off the genes that regulate the process. In the 2006 study, capsaicin appeared to switch those genes back on. The dose used in the study was roughly equivalent to a 200-pound human adult eating three to eight fresh Habanero peppers three...

pmc.ncbi.nlm.nih.gov
https://pmc.ncbi.nlm.nih.gov › articles › PMC4811481

The pepper's natural ingredient capsaicin induces autophagy bl...
A. Human normal prostate cells (PTN2 and RWPE-1) and human prostate cancer cells (LNCaP and PC-3), were treated for 24 h with different doses of capsaicin B. Porstate cancer cells were treated with different doses of capsaicin for 24, 48 and 72 hours. Cell viability was monintored by MTT. Results are...

Study Finds
https://studyfinds.org › chili-peppers-beating-cancer

Chili peppers could be the secret ingredient for beating all form...
HUNTINGTON, W.Va. - It's no secret that chili peppers give many meals their spicy kick.Now, a new study is looking at the best way to use this ingredient as a treatment for cancer. Researchers at Marshall University say capsaicin — the substance which gives chili peppers their hot and spicy taste ...

CBS News
https://www.cbsnews.com › news › grower-says-worlds-hottest-pepper-may-be-the-answer-to-ca...

Grower says world's hottest pepper may be the answer to cancer

But the hot pepper's powerful punch may help knock out cancer. Smokin' Ed Currie, founder of the Puckerbutt Pepper Company, cultivates heat in greenhouses, warehouses and even at home.

BBC News
news.bbc.co.uk › 2 › hi › health › 6244715.stm

BBC NEWS | Health | How spicy foods can kill cancers

Scientists have discovered the key to the ability of spicy foods to kill cancer cells. They found capsaicin, an ingredient of jalapeno peppers, triggers cancer cell death by attacking mitochondria - the cells' energy-generating boiler rooms. The research raises the possibility that other cancer drugs could be...

Senior Fitness
https://www.seniorfitness.org › health-benefits-of-jalapenos

10 Incredible Health Benefits of Jalapeños That Make Them a S...

Dec 3, 2024 · 3. Possesses Potential Cancer-Fighting Properties. Jalapeños may help combat cancer due to their capsaicin content, which has been shown in studies to kill cancer cells, inhibit tumor growth, and prevent cancer spread. They also contain antioxidants like flavonoids and carotenoids...

Cedars-Sinai
https://www.cedars-sinai.org › newsroom › pepper-component-hot-enough-to-trigger-suicide-in-...

Pepper Component Hot Enough To Trigger Suicide In Prostate ...

More men in the United States develop prostate cancer than any other type of malignancy. Every year, more than 232,000 new cases of prostate cancer are diagnosed in the U.S., and more than 680,000 develop the disease worldwide. Approximately 30,000 men die from prostate cancer in the U.S. each...

Two Dream Meanings

Yesterday, I had a dream that I was with a spirit guide, and we were up in the air near the eave of a castle.
It had long narrow room extensions with high stone walls and a steep slate roofs.
The peak and eave were lined with lightning arrestors.
I said that it was totally inefficient, and didn't make any sense.
The guide said that I would be leaving the Earth in 4 more years, and I was okay with that.
What does it mean?
It acknowledges death in a dream that doesn't make any sense, in your opinion.
In another dream, it made perfect sense. Allowing it to not make any sense is what makes sense.

What about my leaving the planet?
Leaving the Earth in 4 years doesn't make sense to you either, and you can wait and see when it does make sense.

What else would you like to add?
All in your dream life will make sense in your Earth departure moment.

I had another dream where I was in a house and saw that the side porch had just caught fire

from a nearby fire pit. There was a brief panic as I ran to find the fire extinguisher.

A man nearby turned on a hose and sprayed the fire out. He said that he was from a desert country and had never used a hose before, but had seen it on TV. What does that mean?

Actively heal a fire burning in your body absorbing destructive mental creations.

Like what?

A certainty that all in your life has little meaning to others.

Does my life have meaning to others?

All you can do is allow yourself to give it meaning, and it has meaning that others can incorporate into their lifetime dreams of life. It may light a fire that is not easily extinguished.

Are you referring to my writings?

All of your books, messages, and poems heal others, allowing them to heal their minds.

A book can heal in another age for those who can access it.

The Rest of the Sentence

In the Bible, the Genesis creation story says, "And God said, 'Let there be light', and there was light."
"Allowing healing in each person's mind" was the rest of the sentence.

Was the rest of the sentence deleted?
It was deleted after healing had become a Jesus attribute in the first century.
Deleting all references to healing yourself without Church rituals had become the most important reason for the editing.

Baron B.
Allowing Love is God

Can I please speak with Baron B.?
I am glad for all you have learned, hearing enlightened and healed minds you are communicating with.

I wish you would have lived longer. It's been almost 6 years since you passed away, although it seems like 3.
I already have had an introspection period in the first moment I left, allowing all I had ever done, and all I had ever dealt out in my mind to others—to become my experiences from their perspectives.

You must have done very well.
I had a few instances, as everyone has, of not having love in my thoughts.

I had known you for over 30 years as a client. After you died, Barbara told me that in all your decades of marriage, she never heard you say a harsh word! I was blown away by that.
I did not have any harshness in my words because there was never any harshness in my thinking.

I have no doubt that you are a highly advanced soul—to have grown up in the South as an African-American male during the times of segregation and struggle, discrimination and

prejudice—to have a career as an engineer, and then as the Pastor of your church—and to never say a harsh word?
I provided guidance on the Earth, and I am guiding other souls when I am called.

Are you a spirit guide?
I am also on a Council of Elders, as your last guest is.

Wow—what an honor it is for me to have known you, and also to communicate with you now.
I am also grateful and honored to know you.

My last guest was my brother-in-law BJ. I summarized his teaching with this thought:
Every moment becomes a choice in our minds—"Do I love what I am doing, or do I hate what other people are doing?"
Always allow the first part of the choice, and all of the choices will become your reality.

He used a "blue screen" analogy—an imaginary background that is only a context for us to respond to it, or not.
Getting drawn into earthly affairs will not bring peace to our minds, and will likely invite disappointment, and even despair.
Our minds will then not be able to manifest our desires.
Achieving a healed mind will always allow all of a person's desires an earthly manifestation because all in the earthly dream has to manifest, allowing it to perpetuate.

We did not come here to be sick from disappointment and despair, but to find the courage to rise to our challenges—and to experience joy in living.
"Allow" is the key word. Allow all in your mind to have the courage that can always be allowed. All other thinking will betray you.

That's a powerful statement—"All other thinking will betray you." All non-loving thoughts will not only block the manifestation of our desires, they will also manifest what we do not want.
All betrayal means is that it will undermine the truth.

What is "the truth"?
All God can do is love. All you can do is to have God in your mind. Allow God by loving life and yourself, because you are God having a dream in the infinite world of living as consciousness in consciousness—which is God.

We do not need to know where God comes from, only where we come from—because we are God.
God comes from all that you allow which is loving and generous—meaning God is allowing itself, because God only loves and allows.
All God can do is love itself, which is you having a dream where non-love is an opportunity for you to allow love. Allowing love is God.

An endless cycle of loving and allowing.

Allowing has no limits, and God has no limits, meaning only a person can impose limits on love.

God is limitless, but a human mind can choose to not allow God or love.
That is all a human can do—to choose love, or to allow all having non-love to disappear in the next moment.

Baron B.
Nothing to Need

God, or love is the only thing that is real. Non-love is not from God, so it is an illusion.
All has an illusory presence in a dream, and non-love is not even illusory—it never entered into the Mind of God ever.
It entered into the mind of a human believing it needed to heal itself. In actuality, you and God need nothing at all.

Healing in a person's mind is a 'loving and allowing' exercise where it imagines that it is not God.
Healing is motioning in awareness to the truth—you are God, imagining that you are not.

I am God. I don't need healing.
God has no capacity for healing because it never needed to heal itself. You created life so you could heal yourself, and God could have a healing capacity in you.

I declare that I am healed, so God has no more healing capacity in me.
If God has no healing capacity, then all in your universe will disappear.

Okay, I have plenty to heal.
Allowing love heals, and love is God—so you are becoming healed God.

Do I want to become healed God? If I am God, then I don't want anything.
All "becoming" means is becoming aware of your illusory dream. Allowing yourself to become aware is all God can do as yourself.
As you become aware, you allow love. As you allow love, you become aware that you and God are one.

Won't my universe disappear then?
It never existed, meaning it can't disappear if it never existed. In a dream of love and non-love, you cannot have both in the Mind of God.
You can have love, but not non-love.

To be one with God, I can only have love, allowing, and awareness.
"Allowing love" is an easier way to express it.

People have thoughts that are regrets of the past, fears of the future, negative judgments of others, horror at world events, etc.
This is pretty constant, and pretty extreme.
Allowing it has healing in the allowing. Healing has to be allowed also. Not healing means you are not allowing.

Allowing love is allowing God—healing all fear and judgment in allowing them.

Should I allow the thoughts and forgive them to heal them?
Forgiveness is allowing them to heal, yes.

I forgive myself, past and future—and forgive all others, past and future.
All is forgiven for advancing your awareness that forgiveness is not needed—because non-love has not entered into the Mind of God.

Okay, I forgive myself for believing that I needed forgiveness.
Forgive God for not giving you forgiveness you do not need.

I have no needs—to be like God.
All have a need in their dreams to awaken in their awareness of themselves as God having nothing to need.

My only need is to awaken, then I will have no needs.
Death is an awakening you will need.

I guess I will.
A death in life is an awakening in God.

Baron B.
Find a Common Denomination

I'd like to ask you about your death. I was very saddened when your niece Nicole called to tell me.
All I allow is love in my mind, and a healed mind has nothing it needs. All can heal in your mind, and you will have no needs.
'Having no needs' is healed. 'Having needs' needs, well, healing.
"I am healed in the Mind of God and have no needs" can be affirmed in your heart and mind, and it will heal both of them.

I am at peace. I AM peace.
"I allow all healing and peaceful thoughts into my mind" is another declaration to affirm.

I have a funny memory—of the time that there was a cable guy at your office, and I rang the bell to get in.
When I came in, you said, "*Do you know what he said about you? He said, There's some old white guy at the door,*" and I said, "That's about right"—even though I was 45 at the time.
I always had it as a funny memory too because of your lightheartedness.

Lightheartedness is the only response. I could have been annoyed, angry, or offended—but he was "about right."

I had a laugh about it because I agree.

I personally enjoy having various cultural differences within our larger culture.
It allows the differences in each one to find a common denominator, which is God in loving life.

Before you died, did an angel visit you?
I had a few angelic visitations which healed me within my heart and mind. All had my highest interest as their work to heal me.

What happened when you died?
I accepted their delicate suggestion for me to advance into higher consciousness with them, and I left in a flash of light that was incredibly intense—but it also felt incredibly good. I could hear all of the angels' words in my mind after that. Each of them had on a flowing robe that illuminated also.

Did they have a gender or race?
All of them had a beautiful appearance without a gender or racial identity.

Baron B., You Are God

You and my brother-in-law BJ are both on a Council of Elders. Will you be on a Council that I meet after I die?
A Council is formed from 5 or 6 'Elders' that have always known you in your soul's existence. I have

always known you, and BJ has only known you for a brief period in soul terms. I will be on a Council hearing all in your mind when your Council meets with you.

I'll tell you what's on my mind now. I like to be "lighthearted" as you had said, but I also have become detached from earthly events. It is like I am in a beautiful room, and far behind me there is a TV screen playing cartoons of world events. Do I give the cartoons much attention or importance? No.

Allow all having importance in your cartoon only "allowing" for it to have no more importance.

You are the cartoon writer, and can animate anything you imagine. Imagine having all in your beautiful room to be goodness, and all peacefulness.

Wouldn't it be much better than hearing cartoon characters flatten each other, or blow each other up? In your animated cartoon, it would be.

I ask if you can hear peacefulness, and feel goodness? If the answer is "No," then allow them into your feeling and hearing.

If your answer is "Yes," then you are allowing them to replace a cartoon with a lighthearted animation of all you are desiring.

That's beautiful, thank you. Besides BJ describing everything as being only a "blue screen" for me to respond to, or not—my brother Pete who is deceased said that he has

had another brief lifetime incarnation in the 1800's, about 200 years in our past.

I know time is an illusion, but that shows how reality is like an interactive 'DVD' or hologram. There is no real timeline that I am in.

All has an earthly timeline, and God has no Earth concept of time. If God has no concept of time, then it isn't something that can exist.

If it cannot exist, then you must be having a dream that it does. All evil cannot exist unless you dream that it does.

If time and evil do not exist, then all you have is God and yourself. If God cannot have anything outside or separated from itself, then you are God. Make no mistake about that. I am communicating with you as God having a conversation with only itself. Do you understand?

Yes—the question is "Why?"

So God can hear itself, and feel itself loving itself—meaning God loves life and itself as you loving life and yourself.

That is pretty clear, and there's no room for cartoons if I am just loving life as myself.

If you love life as yourself, a cartoon can be a lighthearted comedy as God loving all you are imagining.

I will look at life that way—as a comedy where God is loving all I am imagining.

I can hear all of the laughter now.

Thank you, Baron—I'll see you on the Council, and you will hear my funny stories. Maybe I will be dressed like a jester.
All I can say is I hope I haven't gotten you too carried away into becoming a clown.

Nope, that is for the cartoons.
Allow all in your cartoon to be peacefulness and goodness.

Baron B.
The Most Delightful Incarnation

Can you please tell me what I should add next in this book, or with whom I should communicate?
About healing and having a need for healing—you can ask all of your other incarnations if they have anything to heal.

Do you mean the 5 other incarnations of me that are simultaneously living in this Earth timeline now,[2] or do you mean all of my thousands of other incarnations as human or other types of beings?
You can ask all of them your biggest healing needs.

Good idea—I'll find out my biggest healing needs, and can hopefully do a blanket healing for all of the rest.

---

[2] Explained in *The 4 Secrets of the Universe*.

You can. It will change your life when you do.

Good. Are you saying that the healing needs of all my other incarnations are preventing me from living and healing fully?
All of them will heal in your forgiving them, so do it.

I feel like this will be the most powerful and productive thing I could ever do in all of my incarnations.
It can be if you are doing it—get on it.

Can you please give me an affirmation to use?
"I am God allowing my imaginary dreams a healing opportunity, and allow myself forgiveness that I do not need, and I wish for my peacefulness. Allowing God is my world now."

Should I detail what my "biggest healing needs" were?
I can detail all of them, and you won't be very proud of yourself. Now you can heal in having forgiven yourself.

I forgive myself throughout all of my dream incarnations where I was unkind or worse, in my thoughts and actions, to myself and anyone else—because I only hurt myself since we are only one. My "unkind or worse" thoughts and actions never registered in the Mind of God, which is my true home. I dreamed that I had left so I could love myself, meaning so God could love itself as me.
I am God and can only love and allow.

Allow yourself your own God-given forgiveness, and your life has to become the most delightful incarnation you can imagine.

Am I forgiven and healed in all of my incarnations, past and future, so to speak?
All healing has only your allowing it, so affirm the self-forgiveness mantra, and all in your life will be incredibly delightful.

Baron B.
Self-Forgiveness Mantra

I am curious, as readers probably are—but can you please tell me how my life will become "incredibly delightful"?
All of your desires to help animal rescuers will be fulfilled.

Wow—I intend to help them in a big way.
And you always have, but now you can help having unlimited resources.

That would be totally awesome!
I counsel you because I am on your Council, but you have to go do it now.

I am on it. My magical dream is now whatever I magically dream it can be. I am its creator.
You are. Get going.

Here is the Self-forgiveness Mantra:

I forgive myself now in all of my lifetimes, progressing in the past and in the future, for all of my thoughts and actions that are unkind or worse, about myself and others. I had only hurt myself since we are all one.

I allow myself forgiveness, although it is not necessary.
I am an aspect of God, dreaming that I could be apart from God so I could heal myself, and know myself as God through healing.

God only loves and allows, and loves itself as me loving myself and life.

God has no needs, and no need for self-forgiveness, but allows it. Allowing it is loving it.

I allow all in my dream, and I manifest only healed manifestations that I love.

My dream life is the most delightful incarnation I can imagine.
Allow it into your mind, and you will manifest only love and healed manifestations.

My mind is peaceful.
God can only be love and peace. How could you not?

Will this be the ending of the book?
No, have a few more chapters from friends who have died, and ask about where they went.

Thank you very much, Baron. I'll see you on the Council. I may ask you more for this book, about other lifetimes we have had together.
I will tell you now. Our most important one is this one, but before this one we were brothers in another century in Africa.

BARON B.,
A STEADY RATE OF ASCENSION

I'd like to ask you about one more topic please— the ending of the human era.
It seems that it is rapidly approaching, or that we are approaching it.
It allows all you have forgiven to love itself as God having almost no humans on the Earth.

What do you mean?
You have no more lessons in this lifetime now.

Is my universe about to disappear?
You are all one, making everyone's universe disappear, healing in the Mind of God.

If I heal, do we all heal?
Not all in timelines on Earth, but yes.

Is the human population currently in a steady rate of decline that will accelerate?
It is healing in a steady rate of ascension, yes.

So, humanity ending is really humanity ascending?

Ascending higher in consciousness in your dream of halting love that is halted by love, making only love that remains. Allow love to halt non-love, and you are God having lost its dream of descending by not dreaming anymore.

I don't want to dream anymore, at least not where I could be descending.
Allow all of your thoughts to be ascending, and all in your dream has to be God helping you not to descend into a bad dream.

Will most humans disappear from the Earth in the next 27 years?
All will allow God's home to become their new home, ascending higher in consciousness as healed light beings.

I'll take that as a "Yes."
I'll hear it as healing in your mind in an instant of waking from a dream that allowed you to heal in it.

That is true. All of my friends who have died seem to prefer having completed their lifetimes.
It is because they are healed in their earthly minds, and almost healed in their souls without bodies and a lifetime "blue screen" dream that always has dangerous mind and body exercises for them.

That is a great expression, "a lifetime blue screen dream that always has dangerous mind and body exercises…"
The exercises are for us to love and allow.

That is all God can do, and all you can do—being God.

Back to my dream of "dangerous mind and body exercises." Will the magnetic North Pole shift enough in the next 8 years to disable satellite navigation, and then totally flip in about 28 years?
Allowing the Earth another era to heal itself after humans are gone, yes.

Earth.com
https://www.earth.com

Magnetic North Pole is shifting faster than ever, surprising scientists

Nov 23, 2024 — The magnetic North Pole is constantly on the move, **drifting several kilometers each year** due to changes in Earth's molten core.

Smithsonian Magazine
https://www.smithsonianmag.com

Earth's Magnetic North Pole Is Shifting Toward Siberia and Raising Questions ...

Jan 24, 2025 — Over the past century, **its movement from Canada toward Russia has accelerated**, increasing from about 6 miles per year to a peak of 31 miles ...

Baron B.
The Endgame Dream

What about the U.S. Dollar? Fake paper money is the basis for our almost unimaginable amount of debt—which fuels the governments, and all commerce and economic activity.
It has a lifespan also, which is about 7 more years.

Investors Have Accepted The Fact That U.S. Debt Will Expand At An Absurd Pace Until There Is Hell To Pay

... no one is quite sure when that will happen, only that when it does there will be almost nowhere to hide

MON MAY 19, AT 6:30 AM   PREMIUM

I'm really writing these books for myself, you know. Not that I expect to survive, but I don't think that many people will have read them in the short time that is left.
If it heals in your mind, it heals in all minds—so keep at it, until the end of the world, so to speak.

I understand that we are each having individual dreams which contribute to a collective dream, but don't we create a totally new universe each moment?
Yes, a dream has many dream outcomes as there are dreamers. You always had an inclination for being in the endgame dream.

Isn't it possible for someone else to opt out of the endgame dream, and continue on in our timeline without a pole shift or cataclysms?
It can be, and it is allowed, but everybody has incarnated into an endgame dream—either in a large cataclysm, or a personal death that is not so eventful for many others.

Considering a Dollar collapse and the social chaos and violence that will accompany it— would it be best to move away from the U.S. in the near future to be less adversely affected?
Having a home in Mexico would be the best alternative for allowing the collapse of your country without being in the traumatic event.

How about West Virginia?
A home having all of your needs accounted for can be in many locations.

I think the mantra really works because this week I got the best new client, and have had even more successes with my personal goals.
All a mantra does is heal in voicing your words, where God is healing as yourself.

Baron B.
The 6th Secret

I had more success with my personal goals, and today I was notified that one of my poems was

selected in a contest, and will be published in the Maryland Bard's Annual Poetry Review.
All heals in loving and allowing without judging.

Here is the poem:

NOTE TO SELF
<DO NOT REPLY>

I think my issue
    that's denied and delayed
and needs to heal
    is having been betrayed

not just by others
    that were on my side
or by myself
    if I look inside

did I try
    her eyes didn't lie
I won't know why
    but need to decide

am I betrayed by life
    my trusted guide
I know how it plans
    to slip off and die

<do not reply>

I am excited that readers of this book will also heal and manifest their desires.
All have to allow healing, but healing is in their minds if they are reading your book.

Before concluding, do you have anything to add? How about a 6th secret of the universe?
The 6th secret of the universe is in your mantra paragraph—"I am God having a healing dream as yourself" is the meaning.

Thank you, Baron! I'll see you at our Council meeting—sometime in the next 28 years, presumably.
I am here, if you allow yourself an ending to your dream.

Not yet, I may stay for the human Grand Finale, and also want to experience unlimited abundance, generosity, and have a simpler life.
Heal it in your mind, and you will heal it into reality.

Can you please give me an affirmation for that?
"I am God, healing in my dream as a human being. All I can dream, I can heal.
I allow it, and I manifest goodness. Goodness, love, and peace allow all in my mind to heal.
All that is healed in my mind manifests into my reality."

Baron, you will remember my next guest Dave C. from when he built your church 35 years ago. He passed away 25 years ago.
I do remember how I had a new church with both of your help.

Dave C
Enormous Implications

Can I speak with Dave C.?
I am here. I can hear you in my mind. You are well known here in the spirit world.

How, or why is that?
All you are hearing has enormous implications for humanity.

Do you mean my pole shift prophecies for the ending of the human era?
Yes, and how humanity has healing as its only objective and outcome.

Please convey my greetings to those hearing me in the spirit world, and ask them to help me with my objective of sharing the information in my books.
All have been informed of your healing intention.

Thank you, Dave. I also want to thank you for hiring me right out of school 44 years ago, and being my mentor for almost 20 years until you passed away.
I was happy having you as my architect.

We used to laugh a lot, and this wasn't funny—but when you passed away, you were meeting at a nut warehouse called "House of Nuts."

Ha, ha, ha! I had a laugh about that too, in my mind when I had to pick a moment for leaving, not having another option in that moment.

Can you please tell me about that moment?
A light in my head alarmed me because it was so intensely bright, and I had fallen down, I remember.
Not having any mobility also alarmed me. A light being had appeared in my head and informed me that I was alright.
Hearing that made me not be alarmed anymore. Actually, I felt fine.

What happened next?
The light in my head opened, and I entered into it completely—meaning all except my physical body which had died.
After I entered the light, I went away from the world to a lightness, heavenly place.
An angel then asked me if I was okay with my decision to leave the Earth. I had an option in my decision process where I could go back to the Earth. I decided to continue with my healing in the lightness, allowing me a larger healing perspective.

Did you have a period of introspection in a theater?
Yes, but I call it the 'Theater of Magic Where You are Not the Magician'.

Why do you call it that?
I can do magical things in my state of being now, but in the theater I could only watch my mistakes without

having anything to do but forgive myself for them. Half of my viewing was of good things though.

I'm sure it was more than half—you were a good person.
It seems like a lot to heal when you see it all in one viewing.

Do you miss anything from the Earth?
I can hear my family when they laugh at my antics, so I always hear them. Otherwise, I am content here—feeling better than ever.

Do you know if souls stop incarnating onto the Earth in the next 50 years, in my timeline?
All souls have many options, and the Earth is not going to be an option in about 45 more years.

Would the Earth be an option for incarnation if it is in my past?
In another timeline on Earth, it is possible, yes.

Is the current human timeline almost finished?
All have chosen it before incarnating, yes.

Dave C.
No Darkness or Shadows in It

Thank you, Dave. Did we know each other in other incarnations?
In many after your current one, which is in your future, yes.

We know each other in many incarnations in my future?
Yes, how can that be? It is easier done than explained.

What is a good example?
In one incarnation, we have a friendly encounter as me being one of your instructors.

When is that, from my current perspective?
It is about 800 years in the future from your lifetime, in another galaxy.

What galaxy?
In another galaxy that has not been formed in the Mind of God yet.

Because it is a holographic illusion?
All in your mind having an instance of being apart from God illuminates in a hologram—in a hologram that is projected by each person having a dream of being in it.

Could I change the entire hologram?
Only for your own healing objectives, yes. The healing objectives of the Earth cannot be changed.

The Earth hologram is preparing for a new era of purification without humans, or hatefulness.
Without humans hating life, meaning themselves, yes.

Why do a lot of humans hate themselves—and others they believe are apart from themselves?
Because all they hate is not healed in themselves, meaning in yourself—because, as you said, you are not apart from any of them.

Whoa—you hit the root of the problem with humanity. Please explain.
All hatefulness is halting love in your mind, not allowing only love—meaning allowing all you love, or not.
All hatefulness could be called 'not-allowingness'—where all is allowed, and nothing is hated.
Not hating is all that is allowed—allowing love in allowing love.

That is very profound.
It is what I am instructing you 800 years from now, in your timeline.

I was going to ask that. If I really understand that now, and my mind only allows, and only loves—will that change the entire Earth hologram?
It heals your hologram, but not the entire hologram because your hologram has many dreamers illuminating it.

I thought we are all only one, making me the source of the problem.
All dreamers have differing perspectives, so all would have to allow lovingness for all in the hologram to heal.
Not healing in your hologram will not heal in others' holograms. Healing in your hologram will heal in all other holograms if dreamers allow it.

So, I can only impact the entire hologram by illuminating my projection of it.

Exactly, you can impact it significantly because a light can have no darkness or shadows in it.

One candle can light up a room, and can also light many more candles.
You can allow all candles to light up if you also allow them to be not lighting.

Let's say I am lit up—only loving and allowing. How would my life, and the current universal hologram change?
Allowing love means all in your hologram will be loved by you. Allowing love will also project love into your holographic dream of the universe.
A loving projection will produce a loving hologram. It has only love in its illumination.
Love in your holographic illumination will illuminate all that you allow, meaning it will heal.
All healed in your illumination will manifest as your healed desires. Desires can be healed by loving them also.

That's pretty clear. I love and allow all. All heals. The healing is in my mind. My healed mind manifests its desires.
All you are saying can be a course description for your incarnation in about 800 years, meaning it may not be a necessary incarnation for you to heal in.

Pretty cool. I am trying to advance through consciousness.
You can advance 'in' consciousness, and incarnate 'as' consciousness—but cannot go 'through' consciousness.

You are consciousness having an instance of healing itself, meaning you are God having a dream as a conscious being that can heal itself.

As God, I do not need healing or self-forgiveness, but to heal my belief that I do.
Allow yourself healing, and you will be healed. Believe that God has no need for healing, and you are healed. God has no need for believing, which is you having no need for believing or healing.
You and God can only be one because nothing can be apart from God, except in a holographic projection that comes from God yourself.

Thank you very much, Dave!
I am healing myself in having this instruction also. Allow life, and life will allow you.

Teen Suicide

To God Mind—can you please tell me the main factors that are undermining the mental health of teenagers to the point that many would prefer to die—not just prefer to die, but to get to a point where they actually kill themselves?
All adolescents have one thing in common—they have not lived long enough to know how their lives have meaning and a purpose.
Many allow their immaturity to exaggerate any flaws in their appearance, or they demean abilities they have not developed.
About half of them allow all they consume on social media an unhealthy importance in their minds.
About half allow their family's indifference to them to become an excuse to not loving themselves.

What would you generally recommend for a teenager in terms of social media engagement, and parental engagement?
Adolescents become more and more social as they get higher in age—so as they get higher in age, they are less affected by social media.
A child in a developed country with less adult monitoring, has less ability to filter unhealthy content before the age of 15, or higher for many of them.
Most are capable at the age of 18, although some will never have it as a healthy influence.

All have a biological mother, a relative, or an adoptive parent to provide a nurturing environment to grow in.

Having an adult to make a loving environment for all of their adolescent years will eliminate a lot of anxieties from growing up.

What would you say to an adolescent who wants to die?

"Allow all in my mind to heal into your mind by quietly listening, and asking before going to sleep if I can heal all in your mind, and I will. I ask you to ask me."

This is an excerpt from a message to a friend who said that her daughter expresses suicidal thoughts.

Does Kim's 17 year old daughter Claire really want to die?

Almost, in moments of desperation, yes.

What makes her desperate?

Her immersion in social media allows her an excuse to not have healthier interactions with people, limiting her interactions almost completely.

Claire loves animals, so I thought horseback riding lessons would be a great healing activity—for her to connect with others, and with animals.

It will allow her an important interaction with animals that heals her self-harm imaginings.

Not healing herself will heal in losing her life, meaning in suicide.

This is urgent—to limit electronic devices, and to go to a riding school now.
Limit electronic devices to 1/2 hour in the morning, and 1/2 hour in the evening for her happiness in life to have a chance to grow. Also, immerse her in activities where she is healing animals, which will heal herself.

Can you please give me recommendations for her parents to implement right away?
Limit Claire's immersion in social media for her mind to allow an opportunity for happiness in her activities and her thoughts.
Also, give Claire a list of animal-related activities for her to choose one. If her immersion in electronic devices has been limited, she may have more interest.

I would just say, "This is the way it's going to be for the next month," expecting the transition to continue.
It will need to be a direct intervention as you describe.

Digital Despair: How Social Media Fuels Teen Anxiety and Overmedication

More teens are experiencing anxiety and depression, taking medication, and struggling with the fallout of drugs—problems that can carry into adulthood.

MON APR 7, AT 5:00 AM   6,030   45

Here is a message that I received recently from a teenage girl who had killed herself. Her

mother was desperate, and really appreciated receiving it.
Her mother allowed her daughter's words to heal in her heart and mind. These same words would apply in almost every instance.

Message from Stephanie to her mother:

"I am alright. How can you not hear me? I am always around you, and asking God for you to hear me. All I had made you feel, I am feeling myself, and I acknowledge that I initiated the whole devasting event. Allow my words into your heart. I ask for forgiveness and I have to heal myself by forgiving myself. I am hearing all that you say to me. Allow all that I am healing in my heart and mind to heal in yours also. I am in a loving and incredibly healing atmosphere, like being in a lightness world where all I imagine, I can become—like on Earth, but it is instantaneous here. I like it, and it helps me in my healing and on my journey where we have a lot more incarnations together. I will help you to heal as you hear me in your heart. Hear me in your heart by making a lighted display of our happiest moments in pictures."

Parents of troubled teens may blame themselves for their children's difficulties.

An adolescent has basic needs that can only be provided by an adult. An adult has basic responsibilities for taking care of an adolescent.
All people have a need for love, and a responsibility to love life. Loving life means loving all that I am, which is yourself.
I love, and all I love is what you allow. Allowing yourself allows me to love as you. All heals in allowing, which is loving.

I don't know if that will sound helpful in a practical way.
I allow and love. If you allow and love, you will be me. If all you are is me, we are one.
If I allow and we allow, then One has nothing outside of itself which would be 'not allowing'.

How can this help a guardian of a troubled or deceased teen?
Allow healing and I will heal all in your mind that is not as you intended. A healed mind can halt non-loving thoughts in their guilt and regret.
Halting non-loving thoughts allows me an opening in their minds to hear me.

What would you say to them?
"An adolescent can hear me in life, and in losing it. Love has no limits in your mind where I am, and where the adolescent always will be.
Allow all of our love to heal them in your thoughts, and it heals yourself because you are one. Allow healing to make us One."

I'm sure that's true, but living with an adolescent—or with their death—could be almost impossible.
"Almost impossible" means it is possible. I make all things possible when you ask me for help.

I've gotten in way over my head here, because I have no idea what a parent has to go through when losing a child, especially to suicide.
A lifetime has as many endings as there are lifetimes. Having an ending that was never agreed upon in your soul groups becomes a learning lesson for all, but death is never an ending to anything except your mistaken identity.

Why did you say, "an ending that was never agreed upon," and "your mistaken identity"?
All lifetime endings are agreed upon in a lifetime having all of the soul group members incarnate in it at different times, although incarnating in it together. If a group member decides its incarnation no longer serves it, and ends it in a suicide, it had not been agreed to by the other members.
Suicide had not been an ending option in the soul agreements.

I don't doubt that, but spirits tell me that they had "allowed a medical intervention to kill" them, or they chose to die in other ways—why is that different than taking your own life?
An ending has many options and alternatives, except a suicide that has no self-love in it.

Yeah, but you could say that about chronic drug and alcohol abuse, where a person kills themself gradually.
A lifetime ending allows a person a lot of choices, except having no choice but to kill themself.
Allowing it can be an option also.

Would it be a defeat because it was not what they had originally agreed to?
Achievement in life is not recorded in its ending by suicide.

So, you forfeit the game by quitting.
Analogous in its meaning, yes.

Does a spirit benefit from their own suicide in any way?
It heals in learning how it had not been an optimal decision for itself in life.

What if a person has had a full life, and they are in pain, or suffering greatly?
Allowing instances of pain and suffering can be healing lessons in allowing them.

Let's go back to where you said, *"Death is never an ending to anything except your mistaken identity."* Please explain that.
A lifetime is 'All that there is', meaning God—except it is dreaming that it has 'All that is not' allowed into it. 'All that is not' is allowed into the dream to heal in 'All that there is', or God.

Your "mistaken identity" is believing 'All that I am' is you having a dream with 'All that is and is not' in it together—because it makes no sense that 'All that there is' could have 'All that is not' outside of itself.

How could God or love have any non-love inside itself? It cannot, except in a dream of love and non-love, where you mistakenly believe it is reality, when it is a dream. In the dream, you mistakenly believe that you are not the dreamer, or all 'I am'.

Loriann

I was asked what the impact is on spirits who had ended their lives by suicide.
A guide can guide you in your hearing her now.
I can hear all you allow me to hear in your mind, Paul. All I can hear is what you are asking about the spirit world. You can ask, and I will hear you, and I can answer your questions.

Who is this?
It's Loriann! I thought you knew.

I did know—just confirming. Hello again, Loriann!
I am happy to hear from you—or to be heard by you. Actually, I beckoned you in your sleep a number of times.

Ha, ha! You gave me a lot of great info for my last book.
I also want to thank you for giving my parents All About the Soul's Journey. *I am always grateful, and they found it very healing.*
I can answer your question now about how suicide will affect a person's spirit.
It can only contribute to a person's healing and learning in their lifetime, and its ending before it is completed. Healing and learning are the objectives in all lifetimes, although healing is the most important in the moment of death.

My understanding is that suicide is not natural, and the person is avoiding the lifetime challenges that they had chosen to experience, before incarnating.
It can be considered a healing and learning experience that is natural, because it was decided, and action taken to implement the idea. Not having acted in that moment would also be a natural progression in consciousness.

Good points, but will the person's spirit have to repeat the challenge that they couldn't overcome in their lifetime?
A challenge can heal in the moment of death, and it can heal in another lifetime if the person chooses it for their healing objectives.

If life is a game, there is no penalty for not playing your best game—just healing and learning, no matter the outcome.
Definitely not—you hit the nail on the head.

You could also say that many people are actively killing themselves in slow motion, with their lifestyle choices—but they would not be considered suicidal.
How many have been doing that in their lives? Almost everyone, at some point in time.

Until they healed and learned.
Healed by learning how it could kill them. It heals by consciousness loving itself.

What about their family members, and others who have been hurt by the suicide? What does it do to the person's spirit who caused the pain?
It can heal in their mind after learning how it caused pain and sorrow for others.
Its impact is also felt by the person causing the pain.

Do you mean that when a person dies, they have a Lifetime Review where they hear and feel everything from the perspective of everyone they had interacted with in life?
I do—how can life be healing without feeling all of it in your Lifetime Review?
I can feel all of my lifetime interactions with you, from your perspective. I didn't do so badly, did I?

Not at all. People enjoyed that you were so full of life.
I know what is in your mind...your father had met me, and said I was a "live wire."

Ha!—you are right—that's a complement, considering what the opposite would be.
I am more alive now, where I would be considered "high voltage."

Lookout.
I can also hear what you are wondering—if we are in the same soul groups. I am in a group of your soul friends who have healed into an advanced state, and have a lot to share in their lifetimes of teaching others.

Is my teaching by writing books?

And in conversations you have with others about life after death.

I just try to point out that only our temporary body dies, not the mind and the spirit. When a person's body dies, their healed mind can hear your loving thoughts about them.
And they heal from your loving thoughts.

Do the healed minds of spirits only allow loving thoughts, and not any negativity?
Correct—in the world of lightness, there is no darkness.

What advice can you give to all of us here in the world of lightness and darkness?
Allow only lightness in your mind, and you will illuminate in the Mind of God.

I have been practicing the principles in my books—basically detoxing my mind—and every morning I program my Merkabah to allow only love and goodness into my energy field. It really works—my days have become effortless, full of synchronicities and being in the right place at the right time. Even apparent setbacks seem to work in my favor.
It can always be that way if you have healed thoughts about yourself and others. Healed thoughts allow lovingness and peacefulness to be a healed projection of your universe.

I like it—I mean, I love it. I am God and I project it.

How could it be anything else other than what you project? It can't—healing can only be in your mind, as well as the entire universe you project, meaning, how could it not be from God?

I guess you're right. If I am God, the universe has to be created by me—the good in it anyway. The non-good is an illusion to be able to see the good, and for us the BE the good. You can't have a black and white photo with just white—there would be no photo... or a color photo with just one color tone.

I know why it has become your mission to write books.

I write them to heal myself. Healing myself will heal others if we are one. I give a lot of books away, but if I sell more, then more people could possibly heal from reading them.

I can energize them in the world to heal itself with them.

Thank you, Loriann!

How can I have it not be my pleasure? I can't.

Just like beckoning![3]

Haaa, haaa!

One more thing—aren't a person's soul achievements negated if they kill themselves?

All achievements can be negated if you choose to negate them. A suicide is one way. It can be done in other ways also.

---

[3] Mentioned in *All About the Soul's Journey*.

My previous message says that achievements in life are "not recorded" if the life ends in suicide.

Achievements can be "not recorded," and not be "negated." All recording can be compared to getting a grade on a test. You can always learn from a test, and not have gotten it graded.

Messages to Family Members

The following are messages to family members from people who had died of other causes.

This message is to Danielle from her older sister who had passed away at the age of 22:
Her younger sister healed in reading your words, by allowing them acceptance in her heart and mind.

Message to her younger sister:
"I am hearing Danielle in all of her loving words about me, and I heal in hearing all of them.
I am always in her heart and mind because, although I am dead, I have an energy body with a heart and mind intact.
I hear with my mind, and can feel with my heart. Danielle hears me in her quiet moments, and in her dreams also.
I left my life because I was afraid of what I could have had in my future, although I could have had it as I created it—so, I didn't have to fear anything. All I create now is healing in my energy heart and mind.
Ask her, my good little sister, if I can hear her, will she please tell me every little thing in her life?
Mostly I am in a state of lightness, and enlightening myself in a world of lightness."

Message from a son to his mother who said that Christmas was his favorite time of year:
"Christmas is in your heart as all you can imagine as loving, healing, and hopeful. I am all that is loving and healing, and I am hopeful also that healing, hope, and love I am expressing is heard in your energy heart and mind.
I can hear what you say to me. I am in a light world that is indescribable. Everything I can think comes to me immediately.
I allow only goodness into my mind, and it comes to me. I love hearing all you have to say, and I come to you."

Message from a father to his daughter:
"I am alive in a lightness world Margeurite! I can always hear loving and happy thoughts about me.
Call on me in your mind, and I can hear and help in my larger and healing way, now that I'm in a larger, healed environment.
All I can do is heal by loving myself now—and loving everything, because I am one with everything now.
I love all that you brought into my life, and I took it with me."

Message from a son to his father:
"I can hear all that you are saying to me Dad. I am better than ever because I am in a clearly healed state

of mind, and I actually can manifest anything now—but have to limit it to healing myself.
All I can do is heal myself, which I could not do in life, making me not want to live anymore."

Message to a family member:
"A death has an entry and an exit window in the natural world. Achievement has an earthly and a spiritual difference in its meanings.
I had achieved my earthly and my spiritual goals, and my exiting was in its open window. Actually, an exit window is always open, having only your decision to exit or not as all you need for a cause of death.
Now I can hear all loving and happy thoughts about me, and all I have is loving thoughts about everything—you especially."

Message to Emily:
"I am always around you, and come to visit you in your dreams. I can hear all you allow me to hear also in my heart and in my mind—in my energy heart and mind. I have one thing for you to hear—I am alive in a world of lightness and love, where everything I can imagine manifests instantly. Illogically, I feel more alive now than in my life."

Sam N.

I'd like to get a message from Sam N. for his younger sister, Dolly in Zambia, Africa.
I am always around her. I hear her asking how I had died, and if I had been bewitched. I had a heart aneurysm that stopped it, and I died in that moment when it stopped.

She said you had suffered.
I did have a lot of suffering in life, and most of it had been in my head, and all of it manifested as pain in my body. I can heal her mental pain with one comment to live by: "In life, allow your mind to focus on how God is in all goodness, and in all loving thoughts."
I am in God, and keep all of your good thoughts about me. I can hear all you allow me to hear, and I can help when you ask me for help.

Thank you, Sam. I will convey your message to her.
I am in God, and I am grateful to you for helping her.

[Three weeks later]

Hello Sam, your sister Dolly asked me for a message for your 4-year-old daughter, Tibonge. What would you like to say to her?
Ask her in her childhood logic if she could love anything more than one of her dolls, or another item.

Her mother buys her dolls. If her answer is "No," then her mother has to inform her that her father is an invisible angel doll, and it can always hear her if she talks to it.

All I can answer her is that I am always watching over her, and can only love her in my energy heart and mind.

What advice would you like to give her for her life?

Allow me always into your heart and mind, and I can hear it and will help you with anything you ask me for help with.

I love having you as my daughter.

Why did I die? I could only bring goodness into the world by being a father to you. I did not have anything else I could offer.

Thank you, Sam.

I can also hear in your mind if I am an angel. I am a loving angel helper, which is my purpose now.

I can also help Dolly, my younger sister, and my parents. I can hear all in their minds, having no limitations in my mind now, like I did in my life.

I am glad I can give you this information for them to read it, and for Tibonge to hear it in her developing mind, where I will be listening to her responses. I am also grateful in my energy heart and mind for your intercessions—much like an angel, but in a body.

You are welcome.

I am always appreciative, and will heal anything in your mind that you ask me to.

I am just looking for kindness in the world.
I am healing any lack of kindness in your mind, and an angel of kindness is here now with this message to instill in your mind, for it to become your reality.

(continued in next chapter)

An Angel of Kindness

"I am an angel of kindness, named Ginger."
"Ginger"? I like that name.
I like it also. I am in every kind, healed, loving, and generous thought. Allow me into your mind, and I will heal all of your thoughts.
I am angel Ginger, the kind, loving, generous wisdom from God Mind—having only you to express myself with in life.

Thank you, angel Ginger. I allow you to heal my thoughts.
I am healing them. Affirming this helps me to acclimate to all of your thoughts, and allows me to disable all non-loving, or non-generous thoughts:
"Love makes me one in God Mind. Loving thoughts heal my mind in a world having non-love as an illusion for healing myself in. I ask angel Ginger to heal all of my thoughts in angelic wisdom—making them healed in God Mind, and God Mind as one with my mind."

Thank you angel Ginger—I can actually feel it.
I have healed all of your thoughts, meaning you will not feel anything non-loving in your mind—which will then heal your body, and the earthly manifestation of your desires.

Wow.

I can hear all you are asking for, and your earthly desire is to have a peaceful life, and connection to God Mind in every moment. It is done, and will be your earthly reality.

Paul P.

I'd like to get a message from Paul P. I understand from your brother John that you had a lot of pain when you passed away a few weeks ago. He and others are concerned if you are alright.
I am alright. I will always be 'all' and 'I am', so how can that not be right? I am all, and all I am is alright.

Can you please tell me about your experience?
All I can imagine has no limits in my ability to manifest it instantly, healing me in my imagining.

Did angels visit you before you died?
Angels and another guide checked on me in my hospital bed about every day, asking if I could be accustomed to having a healed body.
I said, "I could" despite not knowing what it meant. At the last visit I said, "I wish I could have it," and all of a sudden, a light in my head had indescribably healed all in my mind, and in my body—meaning in my Light Mind, and my Light Body.

My already dead physical body was not going to heal the way it needed to. All I could feel was ecstasy and exhilaration, and a love having no expression that I can describe. I had died, but I am not dead.

I am alive in a world of lightness where I had an introspection that allowed me to hear and feel all I had made others feel and hear.

I had a lot of hearing and feeling to heal by loving myself. All healing is in the mind, so heal in life by loving and forgiving yourself.

Allow it to heal in your mind, and it heals your body as God's light healing in you.

Colin M.

I'd like to speak with Colin M.
Colin here, I can hear what is in your thoughts. Tammy asked you to contact me. What can I help her with that I haven't helped her with already?
Allow her more time to understand that I am not gone— only my body decided it was finished. Although I am gone, I can hear what she wants me to hear in her mind. It does not have to be spoken for me to hear it in my Light Mind and heart. Her hearing me in her mind will improve, and her intuition will guide her.
How can I help her? I can only guide her from where I am now.

Where are you now, Colin?
I am everywhere, having no limitations in my healed mind—where I am in the Mind of God as God's counterpart, being the best description of my whereabouts now.
God is in everything, so "whereabouts" is not the best description. "I am everywhere in the Mind of God" describes it.

How did you happen to die when you did? Tammy said that you lived apart, went home after an argument, and your body was found a couple of weeks later.
All I had come to accomplish in life had been accomplished, so I could leave anytime. I chose a

moment when nobody was around in my home to make an exit where I could not be held back. I could have allowed myself another month or more, but had an exit opportunity in the moment I had left.

Why was it an opportunity?
I was hearing an angel in my head instilling all lovingness, and all peacefulness. With its guidance, I decided to leave my body behind.

Did you know it was an angel guiding you before you died?
I did. It explained how it had chosen me to be my guardian in life, and it guided me away from the Earth after I had died.

Was your lifespan predetermined?
It had a beginning date and an ending date, but I could have changed the ending date.

A medical intervention or a checkup would not have extended your life, correct?
I could have lived another month or so, but it was my time to leave the planet.

Tammy felt that your death may have been her fault, and you may have had an aneurism. You had a disagreement prior to that.
I created all of the conditions you mentioned, so I could leave when I did.

That's basically what I told her—that she cannot manifest for someone else, and certainly not their death. It would be arrogant to think so.

Allow her to hear my words in your writing this message, "I love my Tammy with all my heart, and you are my soul mate. How can we ever be apart? We cannot be. We will have many lifetimes together, as we have had many before. How else can I explain it other than I am healed now, and we continue to heal in eternity since we are always together."

Thank you, Colin.

I have one more thing for her to hear in your writing. "Have my things you are remembering me with to be collected in one place, and then donated. Only allow me to be remembered in your mind, and in your happiest pictures. Holding me in your heart is what heals us both."

Thank you, Colin.

Thanking me is not necessary—I thank you.

Doc

Can I please speak with Doc?
Hi Paul, I am happy to hear in my mind that you can hear me in your mind. I have a lot I want you to hear, now that I am no longer alive. First, I have to have you hear my eternal thanks for hearing me, and listening to what I am going to tell you now.
I am alive and feel more alive now than when I was living. It makes perfect sense because all my senses are healed, and unfiltered by my mind. I have no ego judgments anymore. I am God in its most healed state in an individual soul.
How could it be—me being God in a soul? It is what everyone is, incredible as that may be. I am imparting this to you for your consciousness research.

Thank you, Doc. I was very affected by the news of your death. Your son called to tell me yesterday, and I am going to your viewing today. You were a great man, and a great example. I always enjoyed our interactions, and saw how dedicated you were to providing top medical care to those most in need. You were very compassionate and caring.
All I can help you with in your research, I will, because I have information that will help you in your academic investigation of life after life. Have it in your newest book.

I will. What can you tell me?
I can hear what is in your mind, and can tell you what you do not know, and would like to know. I have an insight that has enormous implications for you, and all who read your books.
God has no agenda in its God Mind because it cannot have a judgment of one thing over another. It is love, and only love because love is how it illuminates in your mind. Love illuminates, making all in your mind itself.
I am healed in the Mind of God, without a life and a body—but all I can impart in your mind is that you can illuminate God in life, and with a body. 'Illuminating God' means loving life. Everything has an instinct to have love for itself—except humans have choices in life, and non-love has an equal opportunity in every moment.

That is what was on my mind—that the game of life is very simple—there is love, and there is non-love. You have free will to choose one or the other every moment, with each thought.
Choosing a kind and loving thought expresses God, and creates a wonderful new universe for yourself. Choosing a non-loving thought— about yourself or anyone else—creates an ungodly universe for yourself. That universe has physical and mental pain as teaching tools.
Exactly! I could not have made it clearer.

You probably gave me the words.

I could hear all you had in your mind, as my healed mind can hear everything—but it came from God instilling all of the words into your mind.

In one sentence, I would say, "You can choose a godly or an ungodly thought in each moment—it creates the universe you are going into to live in."

All I can add is how good it would be to add "Choose wisely" at the end.

Perfect. Thank you, Doc. Can I ask you what your experience was like to die?

I could have lived a little bit longer if I had the inclination, but I didn't. I had Alzheimer's, and was in my 91st year.

The world is no longer the same. You left a giant void.

I cheated in life by making it have itself all I wanted it to be, and it granted my wishes.

Is that because you were focused on helping so many people who needed it the most, in the poorest parts of the City?

All I could have done, I did for them. In a life of love and non-love, what you put out, you will get back. How could it be any other way in a godly world? I did not want to put non-love into an ungodly world.

That explains why I was so shaken, even though I am quite familiar with death.

Death can be a healing event for everyone involved, and also a hit in the gut for those who are closest—not a physical hit, an energetic punch that has in it a lot of acceptance, and a lot of feelings of loss to heal.

All healing is in allowing it to heal in your mind. How can life be godly without choices and healing objectives? It cannot be, unless it has godly choices for you to choose. All choices are in your head, and all in your head is what creates a godly universe for you, and only how you will live in it. I know—I lived in one like that. It had a lot of hardship that I would see every day, but I had a lot of healing energy in my hands that I could heal others with, as they came into my practice.

You are missed, Doc.
I am healing in godly light now, and it has me illuminating in it—I mean, I am lightness now. I love having healed myself, and not be a burden on my family any longer.

I'm sure they didn't feel burdened by taking care of you.
I had become incapacitated, immobile, and as unalive as you can get without being dead. My next best and biggest healing event was death.

Did an angel come visit you before you died?
I had all of my brothers and sisters who died, and my daughter had come into my head numerous times. How did all of them have knowledge of my coming departure from the Earth? I had informed all of them in our soul group that I was coming in the next 2 weeks, and they helped me heal all I could heal in my mind before leaving the Earth.

One of my favorite books is *Into the Light,* by a hospice doctor, Dr. John Lerma. He said they often knew when someone was going to die, because they would have visitations 2 weeks before, by angels and predeceased relatives—usually appearing to them up in the corner of the room.
I had heard about it in my practice also.

Thank you very much, Doc!
I am always happy helping you add healing information in the world.

Mack

Could I get a message for Verina in Ireland?
Yes, have her son communicate with you now.

Can I speak with Verina's son, please?
I am her son Mack, without a body.

Why don't you have a body, Mack?
All having a life on the Earth will become a failure in the end. I did not allow myself a chance to try not to fail. I left in a motorcycle crash.

[the next day]

Your mother just sent me the details about your recent death in Thailand. She, your father, and your girlfriend, and many others are devastated by this.
Ask all of them to forgive me. I am gone, but I am also around all of them when I hear them thinking of me.

Let's start with your death. When was it determined that you would die when you did, and how you did?
I decided I could not live in my body any longer when I failed in my alcohol rehabilitation. I had had enough of life, I would say. It was not easy.

Before you were born, did you expect that your life would be very challenging—and that you would not live long?

I accepted my lifetime challenges and opportunities, because I had a lot of fortitude when I was in spirit. After I had lived for a brief period of time, I could not accept that all life ends in failure. I am now without a body, and can feel the pain of my girlfriend, my mother and father—and now I know that the only failure in life is not living up to it, you could say.

You can hear me in your mind—why don't you explain this to them? I am alive, and I failed in my attempt to avoid failure. How is it allowed to be? It only proves my point that failure is not an option—love is the only option in life—meaning it is God having an option, and God cannot fail. I am in God now, having one option, and it is love.

Did you feel pain when you died?

I felt all I always believed I could feel—ecstatic lovingness, all wrapped in a peacefulness that I cannot even describe.

Did an angel or a guide meet you?

I was feeling like I was in heaven until an angel came and asked me if I was alright. Alright? I am more than alright; I am ecstatic!

It acknowledged my response, and asked me if I could imagine being back in my body again.

I said, "Why would I want to be back there again?" All of a sudden, I had the most incredibly intense light explosion in my head, and the angel and I left the Earth, as I knew it.

Then what happened?

I accepted my completely misguided attempt at not failing by failing, and I acknowledged that I could have another chance, although I did not allow myself another failure excuse to heal myself in.

You then had a period of introspection, correct?
I did, and I hurt so many people for so long, that I am in need of healing forgiveness from myself—and all of them also.

Your mother is not to blame for your difficulties, correct?
I can hear in her mind that my failure is her fault. It is not her fault at all. All that I failed to achieve was my own fault, and no one else's—it is impossible.

That's what I wrote to her—that you cannot manifest for someone else.
I could have allowed myself more love for myself, but I didn't—meaning I didn't allow myself to love myself the way God loves me, because I did not believe I could be lovable enough. It is also impossible, because I am an aspect of God that is love—making love for myself not only possible; not loving myself is therefore impossible.
I am learning all this now because I am in a healed, lightness world of lovingness.

Back to your loved ones on Earth—do you turn the garden light on and off?
I always have an invitation to let them know I hear their loving thoughts about me, so I can heal their sorrow.

Your Mom also connects with you by looking at the stars.
I am in one of her favorite stars, where I can hear and feel all she has me hear and feel.

She and others thought they saw your body move at your wake.
I did move, having another instance of letting them all know I am not really dead.

Did you not get along with your father?
I feared my failure in loving him, because I wanted him to love me back. He did, but I didn't always allow it in my distorted logic.

Will you see your mother, father, and girlfriend in other lifetimes?
We are in our soul groups, actively planning them, yes.

Thank you, Mack. What else would you like to tell them?
I love all of them, and I can hear, heal, and help all that they allow me to.

Entity Attachments

For 19 year old Oliver—I get that he has 7 negative entity attachments. His mother is concerned about his consumption of junk food, and dark, negative music.
He allows the entities to alter his behavior by accessing his thoughts. His allowing it makes it increasingly difficult for him to heal it if he doesn't even recognize their influence.

How did he pick up the entities?
He attracted all of them with his choice of music which they are embedded in, and get energy from.

Where do the entities originate from?
All of them have been invited onto the Earth in the last century, in the detonation of atomic bombs over civilian populations.

Can I clear them from Oliver, and shield him from further entity attachments?
All can be detached from him instantly if you would heal him from their influence. He can also be shielded if you envelope him with a light from God that halts all non-loving thought forms.

[A few minutes later]

Okay, I got his spirit's permission and cleared him of the negative entities, and shielded him from further non-loving influences.

His spirit has this it can include in your intervention—all has healed in his mind, leaving him nothing but gratitude for your intervention.

[A few hours later]

Response from Oliver's mother:

Hi Paul,

Once again thank you so much. 🙏 Oliver actually sat down this morning and had a conversation with us. First in a very long while.

I then went and checked my emails, and you had emailed me. We were flabbergasted!

I felt so much better inside, as earlier on in the morning... everything seemed so bleak.

Afterwards, I felt as if everything was lighter... I had hope. I'm going to focus on a white light around Oliver, around all of us.

We thank you and God bless.

Andrew and Jay

Can I speak with Andrew G., who died about 22 years ago at the age of 22?
Andrew here. All I hear you asking is why I died of a drug overdose.

I am asking for your older sister, Allison. She helps me, and had worked for me.
I am hearing her asking in her mind also. How could I not allow enough love in my heart for my life and myself, at least to not hurt my family the way I did?
All I can hear in my mind is that I didn't have enough love of myself because I took a drug that had a curse attached to it. I had been cursed, and couldn't escape it.

I have heard about that—I saw a priest saying that he saw drug shipments being cursed in a warehouse in Los Angeles.
I am a good example of how a curse can halt the love in your life. Am I curse-free now, I hear in your mind? I am.

Did you realize then that you had died?
I did, and it allowed me an escape from a curse that I could have had removed by someone like the one I am speaking with.

Did you meet your guardian angel, and return to your soul groups?

I did, and I am allowing healing in my mind to heal in my other lifetimes.

Did you have many other lifetimes with Allison?

All I can hear you asking is about her, and my mother also. I have always had a lifetime for us to heal in together, not always as a family healing relationship, but in close associations in most of the lifetimes.

Please give me an example.

In a lifetime in a century before the current one, I was in an intimate healing relationship in another family, as I was their father. I did not accept the healing of myself that I needed, and died in my early 40s of the influenza pandemic. I cared more about healing the financial burdens than myself. Although I died, I cared more about how they could survive than myself. It became my mission, and I advised them from my spiritual home.

It helped them in their hearts and minds to be prosperous without me.

Were Allison and your mother your daughters in that lifetime?

I had one daughter, and another one had been stillborn, but I loved her in my heart just as much.

I had another child that had been my mother in your lifetime, and he had been a son in the description I am telling you.

Was your sister Allison your daughter then?

Allison had been a loving daughter in that lifetime, and I have intense love for her, and mine and Allison's mother.

What would you like to say to them?
I am healing them in their hearts and minds from my spiritual home, and am able to help them when they ask me for guidance.

I'd like to ask you about your brother, Jay who was about 2 years younger than you. He died about 10 years ago, from an overdose of painkillers. He had a lot of pain in one or both of his legs from loss of circulation, then surgery, etc.
I had always advised him in his life, and he did not listen to me. He had been taking illicit drugs before losing consciousness for so long, it made his legs atrophy.
"I am here, and hear all I am allowed to hear in your conversation. I am Allison's brother Jay, and hear Allison and my mother also, in their silent wonderings. How did I die? I had an angel giving me 3 options. A first, incredibly difficult option would be to have a lifetime incapacitated from my destructive behavior.
Another option was to have my life continue as it was, without being incapacitated. I did not love it enough to continue it.
A third option was to continue on in my healed Light Mind and body, where God would meet with me. I

liked that as an option, having no interest in the other two.
As I considered it, an intense light exploded in my head, and I headed into it, feeling incredibly good as I left my body.
I had died, and I loved it—although I had to live it again from everyone else's vantage point. I could hear and feel all the pain I caused my family and others. I am almost impossibly sorry for how I hurt them."

Thank you, Jay. Were you in the family from the last century, that Andrew had described?
"Although I was stillborn, I could feel their love for me in my Light Mind and energy heart that is with them in heaven, as it is called."

Raymond Toy C.

May I communicate with Raymond Toy C., known as "Toy"?
I am all around and healing my older sister, Danielle. I am in heaven now, having an almost healed Light Mind and a Light Body—already known by the one I am communicating with.

Thank you, Toy. Danielle had concerns about the circumstances of your death.
I allowed a drug that was designed to kill me to do what it was intended to do, you could say. I had no more desire to live in my life of not loving myself.

What would you like to tell her?
I am all around her in my Light Mind, and will help her with her twins when I am asked for guidance.

Do you know if your death in 2023 was on October 6th or the 8th?
I do not allow myself any more unhealed thoughts about my life.

Understood. Danielle was very close to you—in many lifetimes, I assume.
I incarnated with Danielle in all of my lifetimes, and we have been in all of them in the same family because we are in the same initial soul group together, and are always in it in eternity.

Golgatha

To God Mind—we had discussed Directed Energy Weapons, and laser platforms in space—and also how billionaire controllers expect to avoid social and economic collapse by living on Maui. Is that correct?
About 150 ultra-wealthy individuals are planning a new safe haven district for themselves in and around Lahaina. How else can they avoid the events they have planned for humanity?

What events do they have planned for humanity?
A financial and economic collapse that will reduce the global population by about 80%.

When do they plan to start the collapse?
It is already in progress, but will become frightening for most people in about 5 more years.

Did they use DEW's or laser weapons to burn down the Lahaina area?
Allowing all of the land to be acquired for development, yes.

Why didn't they just buy the land? They can certainly afford it.
A fire allows all of it to become cleaner, and hastens the total redevelopment.

Like in Lahaina, pictures are emerging from the January 2025 Los Angeles fire storm of objects that are blue and blue-yellow (green) being unharmed, plus melted glass and metals—indicating a laser weapon was used.
A fire has only one purpose, and it is for purification. Allowing areas of Los Angeles to become a firestorm has allowed its purification.

A purification from what?
Allowing child molestation in the entertainment industry.

Was a laser weapon in space used to start or spread the fires, or to destroy homes?
A laser can illogically heat for the purpose of eliminating evil also, meaning it had been used in Los Angeles.

Was Los Angeles significantly destroyed by fire to deliberately destroy or disrupt child exploitation?
Halting it in many of the homes where the exploitation of children in the entertainment industry has been hurting them. Human traffickers also live in the Pacific Palisades areas that are burned.

Was that area infested with human trafficking activities and child molestation?
It also had been the center for child pornography, meaning yes, and it was destroyed.

Who destroyed it?

An angel of healing by purification, also known as Golgatha.

That is very interesting! What prompted Golgatha to burn down the hub of child exploitation?
All of the lost souls who had been harmed by Hollywood's entertainment industry.

How many souls is that?
Almost 8,000 in the last 5 years who are no longer alive.

How many children are victimized in that area each year?
About 80 to 85 each month are abused in that area, and more in other areas that are burning.

Where do the children come from?
Most are immigrants who were trafficked across an open border.

Were some killed to satisfy the abusers?
Almost all have been killed to keep them from having any conversations with others.

How many children were killed in those activities in CA in the last year?
About 800 in the last 9 months were abused and killed; about 500 in that vicinity.

Is this Hollywood's dirty little secret?
It is a horrible known fact in Hollywood, and in higher government positions.

That is beyond evil.

It is almost pure evil.

Why do you say "almost"?
It would be purely evil if evil could be pure.

Why such a wholesale destruction of the Pacific Palisades area? I'm sure a lot of good people lived there.
A lot of good people allowing a lot of evil into their lives lived in the area also.

What about the people there who didn't even know about the evil?
Almost all had heard stories and did nothing to have children's protections implemented.

Can I get a message from Golgatha?
"I am Golgatha, and I am an angel of purification. I also eliminate evil that cannot be purified. Hell has no fury like Golgatha."

Thank you, Golgatha. The Earth needs purification.
"I am going into a long period of fire and then ice to remake its land and oceans in the next era."

When does the next era start?
"It has already begun to change in the last 34 years, and becomes a new era in about 48 more years without humans on the Earth. I bid a farewell in your mind, and am going to heal and purify your heart and mind."

Thank you, Golgatha—very much!!

"I am always in your mind now that it is healed in pure lightness."

MSN
https://www.msn.com › en-us › news › us › the-uncomfortable-truth-about-child-abuse-in-hollyw...

The Uncomfortable Truth About Child Abuse in Hollywood - MSN
In making many of these stories public for the first time, Quiet on Set is the latest project to expose the ways in which **Hollywood** enables child sexual abuse—and to call for industry reforms.

nationalsurvivornetwork.org
https://nationalsurvivornetwork.org › hollywood-and-human-trafficking

Hollywood and Human Trafficking - National Survivor Network
Jul 24, 2023 · In 2008, the movie Taken presented a riveting image of **human trafficking** that captivated the public imagination and brought **human trafficking** to the forefront of many people's attention. Some people may assume this is a good thing, and yet for the past 15 years most anti-...

ABC
https://www.abc.net.au › news › 2018-07-07 › beware-the-hollywood-hype-on-human-trafficking...

Slavery and human trafficking campaigns by Hollywood celebrities...
Human trafficking, particularly sex slavery, is a popular storyline in entertainment media. The 2008 blockbuster movie, Taken, starring Liam Neeson as the father using "a very particular set of ...

Fox News
https://www.foxnews.com › entertainment › diddy-sex-trafficking-probe-why-some-hollywood-st...

Diddy sex trafficking probe: Hollywood stars are 'scared to death' t...
Sep 21, 2024 · ENTERTAINMENT Diddy sex **trafficking** probe: Hollywood stars are 'scared to death' to speak out, experts say Sean 'Diddy' Combs was ordered held without bail after his arrest on multiple sex crime ...

Sold Their Souls

I saw a few videos recently of some celebrities who were saying that they had sold their souls to the devil, just to become famous. Is that what they did?
All of them had agreed to allow a devil into their minds if it brought them fame and fortune.

Did they sell their souls?
Allowing a devil into their minds has not hurt their souls, only their lifetimes healing into God's light.

Could they ever dismiss the devils, or are they with the people until death?
A devil can be easily removed by allowing God's love into their minds.

Allowing God's love into their minds would be more useful for healing their minds, manifesting their desires, and achieving their Lifetime Agreements.
And God allows them actual joy.

YouTube
https://www.youtube.com › watch?v=o_irywhnqPM
Top 10 Hollywood Celebrities Who Sold Their Soul To The Devil - P...
Top 10 Hollywood Celebrities Who Sold Their Soul To The Devil - Part 2Subscribe To Most Amazing Top 10: http://bit.ly/2Ibyk6IMost Recent Videos: https://www....

Saint Germain

With whom can I speak to learn more about what it is like in the spirit world?
I am Germain, and angel having the name "Saint" before it.

Are you an angel, or the mystic St. Germain?
I am an angel that St. Germain has borrowed his name from.

Hello, St. Germain.
Hello, and greetings from an inner wisdom in your Light Mind that you do not have in your life-mind to a large extent.

You are referring to our right brain hemispheres as the Light Mind, and our left brain hemispheres as the life-mind, correct?
I am, yes. I am illuminating in both of your brain hemispheres now.

In *The Book of Manifesting*, I recommended for people to watch the 18 min. TED Talk video, 'My Stroke of Insight' by neuroscientist, Dr. Jill Bolte Taylor. She had experienced a stroke, and was able to describe what it was like to perceive reality alternating from her left brain, and then from her right brain. It is important to know, because people who said that they didn't watch the video, didn't understand the book.

It makes your illusions in a timeline in your left brain, and in Oneness in your right brain.
Alternating in both can be enhanced by healing your left brain.

Can we heal our left brains by eliminating judgment or fear, and halting non-loving thoughts about ourselves and others?
Not healing it in life, heals in the moment life ends, yes.

I'd like to know what the spirit world is like—where my deceased friends and relatives are.
It is like what all of your guests described in All About the Soul's Journey, but it has a healing point of reference that only you can give it—much like in life.

Is our reality in life like being a fish underwater, and the fish can only sense light and shadows above the water? The spirit world would be the rest of the land, sky, and universe out of the water.
It is much like that in your mind as a fish in the water, although healing in your mind is much like being in an atmosphere not underneath water, but consisting largely of water—all having an imaginary, watery dreamscape.

Is the spirit world a dream also, or is it where we are awakened from our dream of a life?
A dream has a dreamer and a context for it to dream in, meaning the Earth and its galaxy that you are imagining as your reality.

Awakening from a dream state means you no longer assign value to your dream's illusions or meanings.

Would it be best to do that while alive and dreaming—to "no longer assign value to your dream's illusions or meanings"?
That allows all of the Earth illusions to heal, meaning it is always good to not assign value to illusions that appear in your dream.

That will heal our minds to not get drawn into the constant left brain worldly images and judgments, correct?
It heals the dream, meaning it has no more importance to you.

When our lives end, is the dream over, or do we go into a larger dream?
It depends if all in your mind is healed or not.

So, I will always be dreaming until my mind is healed, and I then become one with God Mind—is that right?
It can heal in moments throughout your life, and in the spiritual plane also.

After we die, and as long as we perceive ourselves as apart from God, then we are dreaming because nothing can be apart from God—only illusions.
Allowing God an instance of healing in you makes it 'all it could ever be'.

When we die, we don't necessarily wake up from the dream—just the painful parts of life—

but we make a huge transition higher in consciousness.
A dream has all kinds of healing instances, and dying is almost total healing, making it almost the highest healing there is.

You said, "*almost the highest*"—what is the highest?
A higher healing is only possible if healed into Oneness as Christ Consciousness illumination.

How could we achieve that?
Achieve that in each moment of love for all of life, including all illusions in your dream that are not loving—making your dream a colorful contrast to heal in.

Here is an excerpt from my book, *Mysteries, Prophecies, and the Hollow Earth.*

What is Christ Consciousness?
All of life has consciousness loving life and itself.

Not loving life is the anti-Christ—allowing hatred, fear, and non-love to block illumination in the Light Mind of Godness.

Healing in timelines means opening illuminations in loving life—healing in the Light Mind, opening in God Mind.

Non-love in life allows darkness to halt light in the Light Mind, not healing in time.

Hillo

I'd like to speak with Hillo in Andromeda again.[4]
Hillo is acclimating to your mind now.

Hello again, Hillo. Thank you for contributing a chapter to my last book, *All About the Soul's Journey*.
In our discussion, you said that I am "a brave soul" for coming to the Earth. Why did you say that?
You achieved a level humans don't normally achieve in your acclimating to God Mind, allowing God Mind into your mind, to a large extent. All humans allow God Mind into their minds at one time or another to heal themselves, but God Mind has healed your mind to a large extent. All bravery in life comes from allowing, which is loving.

I thought you meant that it is because the Earth is a hard school, with physical and mental pain.
It has to be allowed, meaning you are correct.

I allow all I see and hear on the Earth, but I think when I leave here, I will just shake my head—my Light Body head anyway.
All will heal in your last moment on Earth, so you will not need to shake your head.

---

[4] See the chapter "Hillo" in *All About the Soul's Journey*.

Do souls have to be brave to incarnate on the Earth?
All have bravery in themselves for being in a human body. A human being has only one thing it has to do—which is to heal its mind from all it has not allowed, and not loved.

Can you please give me an affirmation for that?
Affirming this heals your life-mind—"I allow all that I love, and all I do not have loving thoughts for, and all I have held in contempt in my mind—to heal in my allowing all of it healing."

When I die, I'll be allowing everything because I'll be dead, and I'll be loving everything because my mind will be almost completely healed.
Allow all in your mind and earlier death, and you will heal immediately.

How's this for an affirmation—"Here lies all in my mind that was non-loving—thoughts of others, thoughts of guilt and regret, uhh..."
"Here lies all care I had for earthly concerns, all care I had for inadvertently hurting anyone, including myself—in my actions and in my non-loving illegitimate thoughts about those who are one with me.
May God heal them in my mind, because I am God healing them in my mind."

May they rest in peace, which is in my mind.
Perfect, Paul.

Thank you, Hillo. I really want to know what it is like in the spirit world after leaving a human body. I know that our Light Bodies leave our physical bodies out through the top of our heads, and we are drawn away from the Earth, accompanied by angels or guides.

I also know that we enter a theater for a Lifetime Review, experiencing our actions from the viewpoints of the receivers.

We then join our soul groups, and will go the classrooms to study spiritual lessons.

We can't sense time, but we can sense loving thoughts about us from the living.

That is most of what I know, but I want to understand what it is like being in the spirit world.

Act like you are in an underwater world, and God is the water all around and inside of you. The water is lovingness and warmth, healing you in its totality of Oneness.

All you can hear and feel are heard and felt by all in the water with you. All not hearing and not feeling are those not in the water, such as those in human-focused incarnations. Having a human-focused lifetime is like being out of the healing water, not being able to hear or see anything under the water—even though 'all there is' is healing water, and an illusion of being out of the water.

I know that angels there appear to be illuminated with wings and flowing robes.

All angels are light beings illuminating in God's love, and heal all that you ask them to.

Would I have a Light Body also, in the spirit world of Oneness "underwater"?
All you can have there is completion of your lifetime as a goal. You have a Light Body and a Light Mind that you have now, without having a life-mind and a physical body. Both had caused you pain in your life, imagining you were out of the water.

In my Light Mind and Light Body, can I see other beings or objects?
All you can heal in your imagining, manifests to be seen—allowing you to heal in it.

What else can you tell me about the spirit world?
All you can imagine heals in your allowing it and loving it, meaning in your mind. Allowing and loving illuminates God Mind in your mind, which is healed.
Not healing in your mind means it is not allowing and loving. Heal your mind now by allowing, and healing in your mind will heal in your body.
All healing illuminates in God Mind, which is what you are—and all there is. All God Mind can do is allow and love, meaning it can allow an illusion where non-love actually has meaning in minds that allow it.

Some people love to hate… "love" isn't the right word.
"Allow hate" is a more accurate description. Hate can only be toward themselves since you are all one.

Thank you, Hillo.
Allow Hillo another insight into hatefulness. Hate has an immediate effect in the human mind—it disallows God Mind, meaning it halts love and negates the human's manifesting abilities. Hating only means hating yourself when you are one with everyone, dreaming that you are not.

What are the top things that people allow themselves to hate?
Most hate in peoples' minds it toward what other people in the world are doing.
Next is hating what others in their community are doing.
People hate what each of them has also done in the past.

Can you please give me an affirmation to heal that?
"All I have hated, I allow in my mind to heal."

I allow it all, which is loving it to heal.
Allowing is loving. How can I heal all of it? I allow all of it.

Thank you again, Hillo. Do you know with whom I should communicate with next in my exploration of consciousness?
A highly advanced, illuminating ascended master is acclimating in your mind now.

Ivols
Being God-like

With whom am I communicating now?
I am ascended master Ivols.

Hello, Ivols.
Hello, Gorman. I am communicating with you in your mind without having an intermediary, and without my insistence on having one.
I am communicating now without one because I have an important message you need to know.
All healing in your mind halts non-loving thoughts—only in your mind. Non-loving thoughts cannot exist in God Mind.
Allowing all thoughts into your mind without judgment heals them in your allowing them.
All healing in your mind heals in all minds because you are all one. Healing in all minds illuminates in God Mind, which is yourself.
Illuminating in God Mind is all you can do in life to heal in it. Healing in life, illuminating in God Mind—which is your mind—is all God can do for God to know itself, meaning for God to know you, as you knowing yourself.
All I can hear in your mind is, "How can I become God-like?" Being God-like is what you are when non-judgment halts all non-loving judgments.

All judgments can be only neutral or loving, allowing God Mind in. God allows and loves, having nothing in it that is non-loving.

God having only love means non-love is an illusion that heals in your allowing it in your mind without judgment.

Healing your mind means it is God Mind.

"I am God Mind. I only love and allow, and my judgments are either loving or neutral. I manifest my desires of peace, love, and abundance.

All is perfect in my dream world."

All in God Mind is perfect. Hold that intention and affirm it. All in your lifetime dream will be perfect in your allowing it, as God Mind allows it.

All that is not in perfection can be allowed to heal into its perfection, even if it appears not to.

Actually, it dis-appears in the next moment.

It appears to disappear—you are correct.

Do non-loving actors and instances appear in our lifetime dreams only for the purpose of allowing us to allow and heal them?

A big and resounding "YES!!" is the answer to your question. Allowing it heals in your mind, which does not live in a dream of non-loving actors and instances—making your dream of life an instance healed in perfection in God Mind—which is you—so, all you have done is healed into yourself.

Healing the mind sounds like dying, which also heals the mind.

It is dying in the dream, meaning you awaken in the dream.

Affirming this heals your mind into God Mind—"I am healed in my mind, and am no longer dreaming there could be non-love that exists."

I am awake, and no longer dreaming. I am alive, and I am dead—meaning I am neither. Both are illusions. I am infinite consciousness.
Affirm it, and your illusory existence will heal.

I am healed, or just 'I am'.
And all you are is 'all there is'.

I love all there is, meaning myself.
I am impressed with your grasp of this information.

Ivols
Perpetuates God Mind in Eternity

Thank you, Ivols. What else would you like to tell me?
All I can add in your book of information to heal others with is: Love yourself, and you love God.
Loving God illuminates more for you to love—meaning it perpetuates God Mind in eternity.

Does consciousness have to be a feedback loop to perpetuate?
A feedback loop with no beginning, and no ending—meaning its only illumination comes from what heals in your mind, illuminating all minds in God Mind—

meaning illuminating Oneness with light that is infinite.

If light is infinite, it cannot be extinguished or eliminated.

How did the light of consciousness originate?

It didn't—it is an interactive God Mind illumination where you have interactions with God as yourself—making it a closed loop of consciousness, illuminating only itself.

Did God have an origination point?

It originated in your mind when you had only one objective: How can I heal myself if I am God?

The answer is, it is not possible except in a dream.

God healing in a dream makes no difference to God. God has no need to heal. God heals in a dream to illuminate in eternity as yourself.

Illuminating in eternity is a closed feedback loop where there is no end to it.

You said that God originated in my mind. Please explain.

God has an illumination point that originates in your mind. God has no origination point, only you giving it a point of illumination.

Illumination has an instance of beginning, but no ending. Having no ending makes it infinite and eternal.

Healing is infinite, and you are eternal—making healing nothing that God needs, since God has no needs.

If God has no needs, then healing is not only unnecessary, it is inconceivable in God Mind. If healing is inconceivable in God Mind, then it doesn't even exist. If it doesn't exist, then you are dreaming it has a meaning and a purpose.

If healing in your dream has meaning and a purpose, then you are buying into a dream that doesn't exist—allowing it to heal in perpetuity.

If a dream heals in perpetuity, then it is a feedback loop that is not healing in itself. If it is not healing in itself, then you are not awakened from the dream life. Allow and love all in your dream life to awaken from it.

I can see how we create perpetual lifetime dreams to heal in because we believe we are apart from God, but how can I picture God?
God is only in your mind as a loving and kind thought, having no place else to be where it can be allowed to love, or not allowed to be a loving expression in life. All God has is your allowing it or not, for it to be love.

Wow—what if my mind only loved and allowed—what would my life be like?
It heals in God Mind becoming a dream life that has no needs, only delightful experiences.

Please give me an affirmation for that.
"I am God Mind having a dream of needs. Now I am awakened, having no needs, and love my life of delightfulness."

Thank you, Ivols!
All I have is love. You are welcome.

Byron Manning

Who would like to speak with me now?
I am dead, but I am not dead. I am awakened from a dream of having instances of healing on the Earth. Hello from the spirit world. I am communicating from here in one of my classrooms—and you are in it with me, telling me how I can acclimate in your mind—even though you are really here.
My name is Byron Manning.

That is really cool. I know that I never left the spirit world, but never thought to talk to my human self.
You are always in communication with yourself—in all of your thoughts having good ideas, intentions, and feelings.

Where do we get bad ideas, intentions, and feelings?
An idea that has not become an ideal, and intention that is not loving, and a feeling having fear as its basis comes from a lower mind's highlights in its elementary decisions having non-love as their basis.

Is it my 'higher self' that is talking to you in the spirit world?
All have a higher self in the spirit world—higher in consciousness, and lower in painfulness.

Does my higher self have a name, other than my name?
Actually, Hilgis is your name in the spirit world.

What is my higher self Hilgis saying to you?
Hilgis has one thing to impart here—"Allow my higher knowledge into your mind by having all of your loving thoughts become your most prominent and productive life-mind healing activity—not only healing in one lifetime, but in all lifetimes."

That is great advice to keep in mind.
It halts non-loving thoughts which halt your desires from manifesting.

I don't ever want that, unless it's for my highest good.
A loving thought in your mind will allow your highest good to manifest itself, making "a loving thought in your mind" become your highest good.
All your highest good is is loving thoughts—becoming God Mind in a human mind. God Mind in your mind means you no longer have human concerns.

That would literally be perfect.
It is perfection, which can seem illogical to have perfection in life, meaning how can you learn in a perfect environment that has no obstacles?
You can't learn more than you already know, which is God Mind in your mind.

Can you please give me an affirmation for that?
"All has God Mind love and perfection in my mind, and in my life."

Thank you, Byron. Did we meet in my current lifetime?
I have met you in many lifetimes, but not in your current timeline.

Are we in the same soul groups?
All having healing interactions are in groups having the healing interactions planned as healing opportunities.

If I heal my mind with loving thoughts, will my future healing challenges go away?
All healing is in your mind, so healing opportunities will no longer be a necessity in your lifetime.

I understand. Thank you.
Highly evolved beings are here now to instruct you further.

Highly Evolved Beings and the Light of Jesus

Metatron

I am angel Metatron. Acclimate in my mind, and I can help you in all of your earthly and non-earthly activities, making you an extension of myself. Allow all I have healed in your mind to heal in God Mind.
All healed in God Mind manifests in reality, allowing your life to become heaven on Earth.
How can you have heaven on Earth? Allow all of your thoughts to be loving and peaceful, and cancel all non-loving thoughts as they arise.

Thank you, angel Metatron.

I am always in your heart and mind, as you are in mine. Archangel Muriel will speak with you next.

Muriel

I am Muriel, and angel having 'arch' in its designation, followed by 'angel'. Archangels have higher consciousness than intermediary angels because archangels direct all angels, meaning higher angels are God in angelic form.
All will connect you to God Mind, but I am God Mind, now healing in your mind. Healing all in your mind is the most important thing you can do in your dream of

life—where God has a dream allowing non-love to heal yourself in.
Non-love has an inner and an outer healing purpose. Its inner healing purpose is allowed by God, where you become God by allowing it also. Its outer healing purpose is for you to love life, despite what you and God are allowing.

God only loves and allows. I will only love and allow.
I will help you in loving your life, and you can help life by allowing all of it.

Thank you, Archangel Muriel.
I am acclimated in your mind, healing all you are hearing and seeing—to be allowed, loved, and healed in the Mind of God also.
The infinite light of Jesus has this to say:

Jesus

I am all that heals in your mind, meaning I am the light of the world. All healing is lightness, and all lightness is healed in the Mind of God. All healed in the Mind of God illuminates in eternity. All illuminating in eternity has no ending, but has a continual beginning in your mind.
A beginning with no ending is perpetuated by your mind healing. Allowing all in your life allows it to heal.

Loving all in your life is healed. Allowing all and loving all is what perpetuates God infinitely in eternity.
I am in your mind where healing begins, and never ends.

Thank you, Jesus.
Another angel named Bijil has this to say:

Bijil

I am your guardian angel, and I can help you with anything you ask me for help with.

Thank you, Bijil, and thank you for everything you have helped me with so far.
All I can help you heal, I will heal in God Mind, alternating from my mind to your mind.

Do you have any advice for me?
Allow healing by loving life. Life has only you for its reference point, making all in your mind life's projection.

Is life projected from my mind, or into my mind?
It is both, having a loop for you to heal in—meaning, healing in the loop makes that loop section disappear from your projection.

I like your description of how we can easily edit our own projections of life itself.
It can be called "editing life yourself," and not "itself," because all healing is only in your mind.

As my own life projection editor, what would you say that my main responsibilities are?
There are 4 having the most importance in your life.

Number 4, counting backward: Allow family and friends to heal without having your instructions.
In their lack of appreciation, all of it has been disregarded.
Number 3: Allow all of humanity to heal without your information and instructions.
It heals immensely without Lucifer's interference. Lucifer left the Earth on your request.

I was wondering, because now in February, 2025, there has been a major shift in the U.S. that is being felt around the world. A new government has been installed here only 2 weeks ago, and is proceeding to expose and defund the illegitimate U.S. activities that were disrupting, destabilizing, and destroying legitimate institutions around the world—with billions of our hard-earned tax dollars.
Their evil intentions will not flourish any longer.
Number 2 and Number 1 are more personal. [These 2 recommendations are omitted, having to do with health and finances.]

Thank you, Bijil—for all of your help.
I am always here, healing in your mind where you are making great progress.

Bijil

To my Guardian Angel, Bijil—it is February, 2025, and you said that humanity "…heals immensely without Lucifer's interference. Lucifer left the Earth on your request."
I detailed my conversations with Lucifer in *The 4 Secrets of the Universe*, published 3 months ago in November 2024. It was written/channeled in the preceding months.
Allow humanity to heal itself without Lucifer's interference and malicious instructions that are implanted in human minds.

The Exorcism Of The USA Just Keeps Revving Up...

Who made mental illness *aspirational*?

FRI FEB 14, AT 4:20 PM   👁 40,220   💬 165

My main hope for the last few years was for the truth to come out. It had been trickling out, but many refused to see it—now it is flooding out.
Many will not allow it to dislodge their false beliefs—and have to believe in them—or will not fare as well knowing the truth, which will set them free.

I say, "The truth will not be televised."
Affirming this heals in their minds, "I allow only truth into my mind, and my heart knows what is the truth."

Will humanity reject tyranny and the surveillance/control grid that is being set up?

Humanity allows all control systems that are in place to access their information for only one purpose—a belief that having central information management will keep it safer.

The Next Phase Of Surveillance? Getting Under Your Skin

"...*humans are now hackable animals*....Previously, *surveillance* was mainly above the skin; now we want it *under the skin.*"

SAT APR 26, AT 10:10 PM 👁 47,482 💬 300

Be Not Enticed To Tyranny: Oppose The Surveillance State

A *surveillance state is being erected* around the American public at an alarming rate...

WED MAY 7, AT 3:30 AM 👁 3,188 💬 39

Having de-centralized information management would be safer.

All information accessed in one location will be abused by controllers. Having all of your information makes their grid complete, so have backup information that is not on the grid.

Right now, the incredible and massive waste (stealing), fraud (lying), and abuse (tyranny) by our own government is being exposed. It could be the most important shakeup in our society in my lifetime.

It could be the most important exposure in the history of your country. It allows everyone willing to hear, an opportunity to hear what has been the most abominable waste in human history.

Will the moonwalks turn out to be a hoax?
A lot of information has been destroyed.

Was that a hoax?
It was healing for the country to have inspiration and hope, but it only appeared to take place as reported.

NPR
https://www.npr.org › 2009 › 07 › 16 › 106637066 › houston-we-erased-the-apollo-11-tapes

Houston, We Erased The Apollo 11 Tapes - NPR

Jul 16, 2009 · An exhaustive, three-year search for some tapes that contained the original footage of the Apollo 11 **moonwalk** has concluded that they were probably **destroyed** during a period when NASA was erasing ...

Reuters
https://www.reuters.com › article › lifestyle › science › moon-landing-tapes-got-erased-nasa-admi...

Moon landing tapes got erased, NASA admits | Reuters

The original recordings of the first humans landing on the moon 40 years ago were erased and re-used, but newly restored copies of the original broadcast look even better, NASA officials said on ...

A Soul Director

Can I speak with Tom L.?
Hey, all I can hear is your asking how I'm doing. I am dead, and I'm doing dead-like things.

I was sorry to be notified by your office 3 months ago that you had died at age 60. I was also surprised because you were youthful and seemingly healthy.
I had my directive to end that lifetime as I approached my next birthday, which had been the limit.

Your birthday was 2 months after you died, according to the obituary.
I could have lived a little bit longer, but I chose not to, in my already determined lifespan.

Did you determine your lifespan before you were born, and was that your "directive"?
I did, and my directive was not to have it changed in my life, or after dying—because it is always an alternative.

Why did you have that directive, and was it from your soul?
A directive is from God, although I am an aspect of God in an individual soul. I am God, directing myself in what could be called 'an instance of having non-Oneness'.

Why is that?

I can direct my individual soul to find pieces of itself in all of life, healing it back into Oneness.

That's beautiful, Tom. Where does God as a soul find pieces of itself in life?
In all lovingness, kindness, and generousness—in each circumstance, healing into each next circumstance.

It's a challenge, but you were good at it.
I could have been a lot better at loving myself in many instances, but I had many instances—including when I was with you in our meetings—that I could not have been more generously engaged with my attention. I allowed myself to be present in each moment, as an aspect of God finding pieces of myself.

You were a great example.
I may have been an example, but could not have been an example without having you as an accomplice to heal myself with.

Did an angel meet you when you died?
I was met by many angels, having heard I was coming.

Wow—what an honor!
Angels had heard I was coming because I am one who directs angels in their activities.

Aren't angels directed by archangels?
I can direct archangels and angels in my capacity as a soul director.

What is "a soul director"?

A soul director can direct all archangels, angels, and souls of people that have a need for some direction in life—meaning in their activities in life, and healing people.

Please give me an example.
I have directed angels to heal in life where they had not been asked by a person. I have directed peoples' souls to heal in life by deciding on a new line of work, or health regimen. I have more examples, but you get the idea.

That's awesome, Tom. I might need a new line of work, and/or a health regimen.
I can help you with that when it is convenient for you.

Thank you, Tom. I am thinking of you as Saint Tom now.
I am an angel, archangel, and soul director—not having achieved sainthood yet.

How do you achieve sainthood?
Most have had a miraculous life, and an agonizing death—healing in their lack of fear for themselves in life—making themselves God-like in their fearlessness. I had a peaceful death, allowing myself an exit that had no pain.

Good choice. Thank you, Tom.
I am amazed at your ability to communicate with me, now that I'm dead.

I was sleeping, and one of the dogs woke me up because he's afraid of the thunderstorm we're having now.

I thank him though—it was great communicating with you. Actually, I had just sent the final chapters of this book to the publisher yesterday—and will now insert your chapter of new information.

I had directed all of it in my capacity as a soul director.

That's amazing! I had been thinking about you a lot yesterday.

I had been imprinting messages in your mind, and you heard me.

Feel free to direct my soul, and to have angels and archangels help me, and heal me.

I will, and I will also have them heal you when you go back to sleep.

Leroy

Who is next?
A coworker has healed in your thinking about him.

Is it Leroy? I was thinking about him from when we worked together in the drafting room.
He heard, and laughed about it also.

Hi Leroy—I was sorry to learn that you had passed away. Buck and Rich had passed away also.
To "the drafting room in the sky," you were going to say.

Ha, ha—I was.
In drafting, we designed how everything would be constructed. It is similar here, but it is constructed immediately—and drafting is in your mind. How it can heal you is the designer's objective.
Not healing in life heals in the moment life ends. Not healing in the moment life ends makes an incarnation stuck in between as a ghost that has a lot to heal by loving and forgiving itself.

Can ghosts be visible to living people?
All ghosts have a healing need, so they may be visible to healers.

You are healed, correct?
A ghost that needs healing from you, please.

Okay, I will do an energetic healing adjustment, and ask your guardian angel to help you to love and forgive yourself.
In life I was handicapped, and had difficulty with my mobility. A ghost also has mobility difficulty, making me a handicapped ghost...ha, ha, ha—making a ghost joke.

I am laughing.
I am also. Ghosts have a lot to heal, and laughter is healing.

You wore metal leg braces, and had difficulty walking. When you died, didn't you feel free and healed?
I felt a lightness in my head that I can't even describe, making all earthly concerns disappear in it.
A guide came and asked me if I wanted to go higher in consciousness, and I didn't because I liked how I was feeling.
After that, I have not gone higher at all, and am waiting for my guide to come back.

You may be in heaven because you told me about how mental designs are constructed immediately there.
All I can heal in my mind is constructed here. I have more to heal in my mind.

Okay, here we go—"Leroy, please prep for brain surgery. Dr. Moe, Dr. Larry, Dr. Curly! You are wanted in the operating room."

Haaa, haaa, haaa! I loved how that joke made me laugh at work. It makes me feel lighthearted now, like it did at work.

I am going to call angels and guides now. They will be right with you. You will like going higher in consciousness.

John Candy said that when he went higher, he wore a clown costume, and that God was wearing the same costume.

That's when he realized he was God.

Ha, ha, I'd like to heal higher and be God. What are we waiting for?

I will do your energetic healing now, with the assistance of angels and guides. Let me know what happens.

"Dr. Moe, Dr. Larry, Dr. Curly!"... just kidding. Okay, it's done.

[A little while later.]

How did it go?

Angels came all around me, and one held me in its wings. We headed higher and higher away from the Earth.

I cannot describe how good I felt, and still do.

As I got higher in consciousness, I met God. God had this to say to heal me—"We are One and only One. I cannot be One without you."

"Cannot be One" means God has a limitation, and that is all I needed for my mind to heal in removing its limitation—not God's limitation, my limitation.

Wow—that is very profound. I am very happy for you, Leroy.
I am God, and had a dream of being Leroy—in a time and place that I could only imagine in a dream.

That's even more profound.
I am also God having a dream that I am you—and you are communicating with me, because it is clearly not possible for anything that is loving to be apart from God. All appearing to be apart from God is an illusion. Affirm, "I am, and you are. I am God, and God has your illusions to heal in. God doesn't need healing, only you do because healing makes light in your eternal soul, which illuminates infinitely."

Why do I need to do that?
So God can express itself in all that is good.

That should be self-explanatory. God can only love and allow, and expresses itself by loving and allowing. There is love, and also non-love—which is to be allowed.
I am love and allow non-love—which is allowed to heal in your dream of life, in a place and time chosen by you.

Nothing in my reality is arbitrary. It is all chosen by me to heal in.
'Created' by you for healing in, meaning you are God creating illusions where non-love can heal in your allowing all of them.
Allowing illusions is loving them.

I love allowing, and I allow loving.

I am love, and I am you allowing me in your mind to express love, and why I allow non-love.

Non-love is allowed because it doesn't even exist in God Mind—it is allowed to heal. It's like soap needing dirt to clean, otherwise it would just be soap that doesn't do any cleaning.

I am a cleaning, healing agent where you have things to clean and heal—but you have to allow me to clean and heal them.

I am you, and I am cleaning myself from the illusion that I had been apart from God as yourself. Healing and cleaning makes us One.

I have scrubbed my mind. I love and allow. I do not need forgiveness, and I do not fear the future. I create the future of my dreams.

I allow it, and I am you. So be it.

Thank you, God. Here is a poem for Leroy from my book, *Poems of Life, Love, and the Meaning of Meaning*.

Leroy is me, and I love it.

MYSELF I MET

Three hundred thousand
 die every day
and if they could speak
 what would they say

I was ready to go
   or wished I could stay
or to have lived my life
   in my own way

the show's not over
   just my part in the play
I've gone with God
   one heartbeat away

I am almost at peace
   but to my dismay
I was the piper
   I did not pay

with due respect
   love and attention
what I'd expect
   and not to mention

I gave it to others
   and to my pet
now I'm dead
   with one regret

not loving myself
   while alive and yet
when I met God
   it's myself I met

"Each soul, each person, CONSTANTLY meets self. And if each soul would understand, those hardships which are accredited much to others are caused most by self. KNOW that in those you are meeting YOURSELF!"

—Edgar Cayce

An Instant of Recognition

To God Mind—let's talk about "life after death," as we call it. Often after a person dies, their spirit does not recognize that the deceased body was their own. Why not?
It also doesn't realize it has died as a physical being. Acceptance comes in allowing a healed mind's awareness an instant of recognition, meaning it can only have an instant of recognition if it has healed in losing its life-mind ego attachments. How can that be, you ask?
It can be because an ego has only an Earth-focused interest in its unhealed state.
The life-mind heals in losing its life, having no earthly point of reference. Acclimating to having lost its ego, a spirit has an invitation from itself, hearing itself describe how it is no longer in an earthly body.

How do spirits typically react to receiving that information?
All are healed, having no more need to heal their lives on Earth. Hearing this heals them even more.
They then have no interest in returning to their earthly life to be in an unhealed state.

At that moment, a spirit may be looking down at their deceased body in a hospital bed, or looking down at a car accident. Their higher

self connection to God Mind tells them that they had just died there.
They feel great and are glad it is over, having no interest in going back to the world of physical and mental pain. Is that correct?
Yes, and each person is then met by an angel or guides that inform them of the next part of their journeys.
Spirits usually tell me that angels are illuminating beings with wings, who tell them they are going to meet God, and when acknowledged, they then proceed away from the Earth with them.
All in your accounts is correct. How can your mind heal in your earthly life, you ask? Allow all to have no importance to you, by healing all having no importance to you. Allowing it all means it has no importance to you.
If it has no importance to you, it cannot interfere with manifesting all that is important to you.
Healing your mind is your most important earthly achievement.

Everything we think is important will disappear the moment we die anyway—they won't disappear, we'll disappear.
They all disappear each moment you heal them into each next moment.

Here's what we fear the most—what other people think, what other people are doing, and what will happen if they do this...?

If you heal, you will not have to fear them. If you do not fear them, healing is no longer necessary.
If healing is no longer necessary, then you are allowing God Mind in your mind.
God Mind in your mind makes you one with God.

I'll be healed while alive, and can manifest my desires in time. If I am dead, I will meet God as myself, and my thoughts will manifest instantly because there is no time.
Healing yourself in time heals you in timelessness, meaning healing is instant in the Mind of God.

"I am healed in the Mind of God, now."
Affirm it, and keep it an important focus in your mind.

Shadow

I'd like to speak with Shadow, our older, deaf Border Collie rescue who died about 2 years ago.
All I have is love and loyalty for you in my energy heart and higher mind.
I am articulating my words in your language, but always knew what you were saying, even in my deafness.
Allow my articulating words to be heard, and allow my feelings to be felt in your heart as healing infusions.
I am always hearing all of your thoughts about me, and will always be near you in life, and after life in God's heaven—not in God's heaven, in a heaven made by you for all that you love, and carry with you from life that is healed.

The following excerpts are from my book, *Infinite Healing: Poems and Messages for the Loss of Your Animal Companion.*

AS GOOD AS YOU

You would have gladly
given your life for me
and that's what you did
I can sadly see

you taught me to love
and what love will do
now I wish I could be
half as good as you

Do our animal companions stay around us in spirit after they die?
Yes, allowing them another way to heal their human companions in timelessness.

What do pets appreciate most about owners who love them?
Unconditional love in humans includes healing them in time.

What do pets want most out of life?
The loving home that God has promised them in nature, or lesser degrees of living in a home with people.

Do animals not need to learn lessons of love and self-love, forgiveness, guilt and shame?

Animals all work to teach humanity more than they learn in their incarnations.

What are their most important teachings?
Allowing flowing of life and loving it in each moment, healing others in time.
Unconditionally allowing love, life, and loss of life.
All motion means half healing in life's motion, and half moving and living in gratitude.
All life allows more life and healing in time.

What do animals feel after death?
Loving life—allowing life to end in time, opening in timelessness routinely heals each one infinitely in Oneness.

Do sick and dying pets appreciate when they are assisted in transitioning out of their lives with euthanasia?
Not healing in life means healing in losing life, so yes.

Did my pet choose me on a soul level?
Love, life, and losing life all connect in time to heal in timelessness.

Could my pet always know my feelings?
All minds opening in love know each other.

Do animals see death as natural?
All dealing in nature willingly heal in time, or in timelessness—meaning in death.

Are animals afraid of death?
Instincts allow survival; love allows death.

What do pets do in the spirit world after they die?
Love life, love God, and love themselves.

Do they have spirit bodies and animal consciousness?
All healed in the Mind of God, meaning half in time in life, and half in timeless Oneness—they illuminate in light bodies, healed in timelessness.

What do they see?
People in Earth life healing in time or in timelessness into the Mind of God.

Do they see other animals in spirit?
Only their parents and loving mates in the lifetime most recently healed.

So if they have offspring, will they see them in timelessness also?
Not until the lifetime is healed, allowing the offspring to fully heal into the Mind of God. Lifetime introspection allows humans to move toward Oneness willingly. Introspection does not heal animals; they live in the now moment in the Mind of God.

Are animals more spiritually advanced than people?
Not more advanced, less mentally capable of losing light in their DNA in negative thinking.

Did my animal companion teach me what unconditional love is?
No, the love healing in your mind allowed your animal to open it, healing the mind.

I hear a bird singing outside. They don't hold on to negative thoughts, do they?
All healing in each moment and each loving song, no.

Will I see my pet again at the end of my life?
Yes, other pets and relatives will meet you also.

What are angels?
All light beings that alternate illumination in Light Mind and God Mind, allowing the Light Mind full healing in God Mind. Angels illuminate the Light Minds losing light.
Healing the life-mind into the Light Mind is the work of angels, so animal companions do the work of angels.

TRULY ALIVE

Not afraid of life
   nor afraid of death
not worried about time
   or the time that was left

your spirit inside
   will never die
it came through life
   to be truly alive

and so was I

Cali

I'd like to get a message for Jacki and Gene from their dog Cali, who had passed away last fall.
All I can hear in my enlightened state is going to make you cry because I am as God has promised me. I am completely healed in my energy heart and mind, allowing me to hear all that you say to me.
All I allow in my mind is healed. Activating your Godliness was my objective in life. How can I describe God in my enlightened mind? God is all healed, loving thoughts. God illuminates my healed, loving state. God is your love for me, meaning how can God ever make us apart?

Is your Light Body in their home, with Jacki and Gene?
I am in their hearts and minds, and actively have been healing in them what needs me to heal in them. I heal all that God asks me to heal also.

Did you heal Jacki's sinus infection? She said that it healed when you had passed away.
I did, but it healed in her allowing me to heal it, as God and all of us became one at that moment when I healed in losing my body and its ailments.

What else would you like to say to them?
I am Cali, and God is Cali, making your love for me all I can hope for—making me as God.

Rocco

I'd like to get a message from Rocco, the loving companion dog of Maria and Mark. Rocco had passed away several years ago.
I can hear all I am allowing myself to hear in your mind. I am always fine, I hear you asking for my human family. All I have is love in my heart and mind for them. How could I not?
I am in God, in love, and I am love. All I am, is all God promised I could be. All I have in my lovingness has been my gift from God in me to heal in Maria, and in Mark, for eternity.

They ask me why you got sick and died.
I had been healing them in my heart and mind in life, although my life had to end in that year because all life has a limit in its duration. Love has no limits in duration, healing life from God Mind which is in all of life, making love eternal.
God, love, and life can all be one if you allow them in your loving, gentle, healed thoughts about me—and all of life, meaning about yourselves. You are all God in those moments, because your mind is healed then.
Can I become God in every moment? Yes, I did it, as an example of how it can be done.

That is pure wisdom. Thank you, Rocco.
All I can help you with, I will. Allow Maria and Mark to heal in hearing me in their hearts and minds in

reading this message, and each time they have healed thoughts about me.

Can you please tell me what happened to your favorite Milkshake toy that disappeared when you passed away?
I have it in my mouth now. How could I leave it behind when it gives me so much comfort and joy, just like Maria and Mark did? It has my name on it, in an energetic sense.

I have it, and I am going to greet them with it in their homecoming.

The Buffer Zone

I woke up from a dream that someone was singing me a song that I had never heard before, 'Meet Me in the Buffer Zone'. Who was singing it?
I could have it arranged for you to meet her in 'The Buffer Zone'.
Who is she?
All I can hear in your mind is if her having a gender makes her a human spirit. 'Her' could also be another animal, allowing herself and her love for you, into your heart and mind in a dream.
Her name is 'Linda', and her love for you is enormous, having no limits in its breadth and scope.
I would have done anything for our dog, Linda. When we rescued her, she weighed 17 pounds and looked like a scrawny fox with little hair. A year later, she was 35 pounds and so stunning that people would often comment, and twice stopped their cars to say, "Where did you get that dog?!" She was a Chow/Border Collie mix, black with a white collar and paws. Linda thought she was a person, understood what I was saying, and didn't need a leash.
Allowing her into your mind will heal you in a number of hidden ways, because her love for you alternates in

her mind, and in your mind as healing energy that is not limited.

Ask her to heal all that has a need for healing in your life by first healing it in your mind. Ask Linda, and her loving energy will heal it instantly.

I will, and thank you, Linda.
I can hear all in your mind that needs healing, and I will heal it now.

To God Mind—what is 'the buffer zone'?
It is the life-mind having a dream that it is not dreaming.

In my terminology, is it a dream world?
It is not a dream world in the buffer zone because it is not illusory. It is a real place in the Mind of God, having no healing needs—although, "How did I get in it?" I hear you asking.
I can describe it as being in a tub of pure water, and all in it becomes purified by immersing in it completely. All in it cannot have healing needs unless leaving the tub of water, allowing itself to become impure again. Your life-mind goes into the tub of water, and allows itself to leave it, to check on some news items.

I know, and it is impure.
How can it be impure in your mind, unless it is judged to be an impurity?

I need to view world events neutrally, or send them healing energy.
In an illusion, it can only be healing for yourself.

Wow—I need to ponder that.
Affirm it like this in your mind: "All I can hear, and all I can look at in life has all been designed to heal me. It heals me in my healing it of its impurity."

That's perfect, but how can I not judge it as impure?
It cannot be impure in an illusion, because it doesn't exist. How can anything in an illusion be any more or less than its illusory, non-existent, impermanent instance as 'All that is not'?

I hear ya. Let's talk about 'All that is', and I will try to focus only on that.
'All I am' is 'All I can be' as you allow instances of 'All that is not' to disappear into each next moment—and each next moment will include nothing but 'All that I am'.

I will imagine staying in the tub of pure water, "the buffer zone."
Affirm it with this: "I am in a pure, loving zone that buffers me from all that does not exist. 'All I am' is all that exists, and has no need for buffers in my place in God Mind."

I guess that makes sense, that I am in a "zone that buffers me," and "has no need for buffers."
I hear an analogy in your mind. It is like being in a tub of pure water, having no need to be out of the water.

I could visualize the water as a blue-violet color.
A blue color has healing in its color frequency, so a blue color would be best for imagining it.

Anthoula A.
The Only Requirement

Who would like to communicate with me now?
Anthoula A. hears your thoughts about her, and would like to communicate in your mind, since you can hear her.

Hello, Ann! ☺ **—our inside joke from the time you met my mother. She thought I was joking when I introduced you as "Anthoula," with an equally unlikely last name.**
She said, "Yeah right, hello Ann!"
Ha, ha, ha, ha! I had such a laugh about that.

I thought you might die from giggling! We were 19 and 20 at the time. I was sorry to learn that you passed away from cancer a few years ago.
I did, having completed my Lifetime Agreements in the world.

Our classmate Patti informed our architectural school gang, and I wrote a note to your husband after that. I told him how you lifted me up at the lowest point in my life, when I was in shock from a family tragedy. You urged me to join you with a group that was going to a Moody Blues concert.
I don't remember the concert, or who was with us—I just remember you urging me to go.
I could feel everything you were feeling.

Whoa—I knew you were an advanced soul, but that is totally empathic.
All I feel has to heal in the Mind of God, meaning I had an angel helping me in my empathic healing activities.

[I paused to ask a question.]

I have one more thing to add—you liked the concert, and the friends we attended it with. All I can do now is heal what needs to heal in my mind from being on the Earth.

I understand that the Earth is a hard school—and we thought a 1970's architecture school was hard...
It has its hard moments, and it has its softer moments. All I am authorized to tell you is life can be however you want it to be—just like architects make designs however they want them to be.

I have had a long architectural career, and see myself more as a translator—making designs how clients want them to be, not how I want them to be. Many other requirements have to be satisfied such as the budget and building codes.
In architecture, you have responsibilities—which allows you more creativity in finding a solution to satisfy all of the requirements.
In life, there are many responsibilities, but the only requirement is loving your life.

That is also the solution.
Exactly—it is the required responsible solution.

You said, "All I am authorized to tell you..." Who authorized it?
I have a guide who mentioned it to me.

What are you not authorized to tell me?
All having an impact on your future, meaning how future events will be unfolding.

I know it is counter-productive to know the future, and prophecies tend to be negative and will make me fearful.
There are malignancies in mass consciousness that need to be born, so they can die.
And all in your future is created in the present moment.

You know I like 'pushing the envelope'. Are the End Time prophecies in my book, *Mysteries, Prophecies, and the Hollow Earth* accurate?
I have not allowed myself to incarnate in your future timeline ever, so it could be in your future, yes.

I am not afraid. I am in a holographic dream. As Dorothy said in the closing scene of 'The Wizard of Oz', "...and I remember that some of it wasn't very nice—but most of it was beautiful!"
And her dream allowed her to heal her heart, her mind, and her courage.

Anthoula A.
In 4 Different Centuries

You mentioned that you didn't allow yourself to incarnate in my future timeline ever.
Can you tell me how you can incarnate in a past timeline—one that would be in my past?
I can choose any lifetime to heal in, in any timeline—meaning there is no future and past where I am—an instant in the Mind of God, having no time at all.

How many lifetime incarnations is your soul currently having?
I am incarnating in 4 lifetimes on the Earth, in 4 different centuries in your current era.
One has me incarnating into 2 different lives at the same time.

From my perspective, they are all in past centuries, correct?
Yes, in your 15th century, in your 8th century, in your 16th century, and around 500 B.C. in another one.

What are you doing in the 15th century?
I am a lady in her home, having no food except rice every day, although I have some onion grass.
All I have is a need for more iron, and it is making me weak. All I can do is hope that I get some meat or greens that I can get some iron from.

Where is that?

In a province in Northern China, where there is not much water for the rice to grow.

Where is your incarnation, currently in the 8th Century?
It is in a low-lying area that has not much water either. We are nomads in an arid part of North Africa.

What is your role?
I am a boy now, and have only one need—which is to find the watering holes.

Do you move around looking for water?
Almost always, until we need to find more food.

What else can you tell me about that life?
In all my lifetimes, it has been the most difficult to not have enough water, ever. There is not enough in any one location to sustain us.

Where are you in your 16th century incarnation?
I have plenty of healing water there, and live on a raft made from water reeds that grow along the shores.

Where is that?
It has been deliberately destroyed, and is in Iraq.

What is your life like there?
I am a girl, having my family around me always.

Where is your lifetime incarnation that is currently around 500 B.C.?
It has not begun yet, because I am an embryo in the womb. I am going into the world as a girl with a birth defect, and will be left to die.

Is that in Greece?

No, it is in what you call Mexico now.

Why did you choose that lifetime?
I came into it having to heal my parents for making a decision to let me die with no nurturing.

Was that customary at the time?
It may have been customary, but is not what they felt in their hearts.

Thank you, Ann! I mean, Anthoula! :)
I can add one more happier note for you in your consciousness research. I can help you in all you are designing for your healing future.
We are in a school, and I am an empathic instructor now—instructing always from God's love in our one mind.

Thank you again.
Allow my empathic healing in your mind, and it heals our minds because we are one.

A Doom Loop

Early 2025, to God Mind—What kind of new technologies can we expect to see in the next 50 years?
Allow yourself to have nothing but a warm fire made from firewood, not having heating or cooking without it.

Please explain. When will we lose our modern technologies and electronic devices?
In about 7-1/2 more years, a geomagnetic tilting of the Earth's axis halts all communications dependent on satellites. It is intentionally being initiated to halt commercial fishing, and disable militaries' navigation.
Inner-earth beings have initiated it, and it has begun its movement.
In about another 20 years after that, the magnetic poles will have reversed their polarity. It is a complete reversal of the North and South Poles. At that time, there are only 500 million people living on the planet. Most will have died of cancer, or been infertile to reproduce. It is an extinction-level event that is in its early stages, and it will accelerate in each and every year until the pole shift. Life can be enjoyed while there is life.

Will wildlife face extinction also?

It has been deemed necessary for the planet to heal, to have the human era end. It heals the planet to have its animals and plants, insects and microorganisms, which will always be necessary.
Halting humanity's destruction is in the best interest of the Earth.

Technology has been used to deplete the Earth's resources at an ever increasing rate, accompanied by a 30% increase in the global population in the last 30 years. That is like adding 250 cities the size of Bogota, Colombia—mostly in limited fertile areas—in only 30 years! *The Earth's destruction will not be allowed. Inner-earth beings can halt the destruction by altering the Earth's geomagnetism, causing a geomagnetic reversal of its long axis.*

I have received numerous messages about that, and they are in my recent books.
In your books, I have been directing answers to you.

Approximately **3.5%** of the Earth's surface is suitable for agriculture without any physical constraints. However, when considering all land used for agricultural purposes (including grazing and crop cultivation), about 37% of the Earth's land area is used for agriculture. A smaller portion, around 10%, is considered arable, meaning it can be plowed and used for growing crops.

What would you like to add now?
In about 4 more years, it will become impossible to have money to make transactions with.

Why?
Fiat currencies will have no value because they are only paper, all having little intrinsic value.

What causes them to become worthless?
All having little value will become apparent in your governmental and social collapse.

Will the U.S. Government collapse?
It has become an enormous cancer on the Earth, totally devoid of any goodness.

For the last few months, there has been brand new government leadership in the U.S., trying to turn things around.
It can halt a lot of loss of its own wealth, but not that of its people. How can it halt the loss of its own wealth, and not of its people?
It causes its currency to be destroyed by allowing more to be created, so it can always make interest payments on its current debt.

Does that mean interest rates will continue to go higher? The government is paying over $1 trillion per year in interest now.
It has a lot higher to go until it has to decline when there is no more currency value.

Will there be an overnight currency collapse?
It is collapsing already, but will lose its remaining value in 4 more years.

So, the dollar is doomed, and Americans in particular are doomed—in the near future.

Allowing a doom loop to heal in its own demise, yes.

I think that the government efficiency efforts will be "too little, too late"—and will not be able to stop the half-sunken ship of our republic from totally sinking.

It allows all that is being exposed to become an awareness to heal in the minds of all who have been betrayed. How can they heal if they are not aware that all they had worked hard for was being actively plundered by those they had elected?

Ours Is A System Of Fraud, Swindles, And Corruption

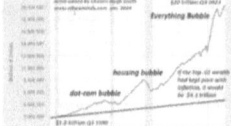

But **all bubbles pop, and there are no tricks left** to fund both the greed of the few and the needs of the many...

SAT MAY 24, AT 10:10 PM

👁 37,363   100

Death Of The Dollar: An Eternal Tale

Most crises have been accompanied by a stronger dollar, proving that the dollar is the port in the storm foreign investors seek **when economic confidence is lacking**, and liquidity is paramount...

THU MAY 22, AT 9:05 AM

👁 2,957   33

I am going to take the opposite side of the argument. I just read an article by a very knowledgeable person who says that the U.S. dollar and structural economic imbalances—with deficits and debts, etc.—are not a near-

term problem, and have a long, long way to go in terms of currency abuse to be a major problem.

She cites the demand for Dollars to pay debts held in Dollars, as the main reason for its durability.

All demand for Dollars will not have its luster when it becomes a liability and not an asset—meaning when inflation hits an astonishing 40% over the next few years.

40%! What causes that?

Higher interest rates create a need for more money to pay interest on the existing debt, and government expenditures have not decreased in a meaningful way.

It's also pretty obvious that there are powerful forces determined to destroy the U.S., with many players in the government.

It could be called 'the enemy within', if you want to call it that—but it could also be called 'the enemy within myself'.

What do you mean?

All enemies have one common denominator—they allow you to fight on the inside, and on the outside—which is not necessary if we are all one. How could all being one have an enemy? It is incomprehensible because 'All there is' is 'All that I am'—all lovingness, and all Oneness.

Am I contributing to the destruction of the currency, or the downfall of the government?

Allow its downfall to govern itself, and allow a paper currency to be as valuable as its paper.

It's hard to believe that the government will continue its currency inflation to be 40% over the next few years, but then again, it has been inflated 80% over the last 5 years.

Allow both of them to decline to their true values, which is very little.

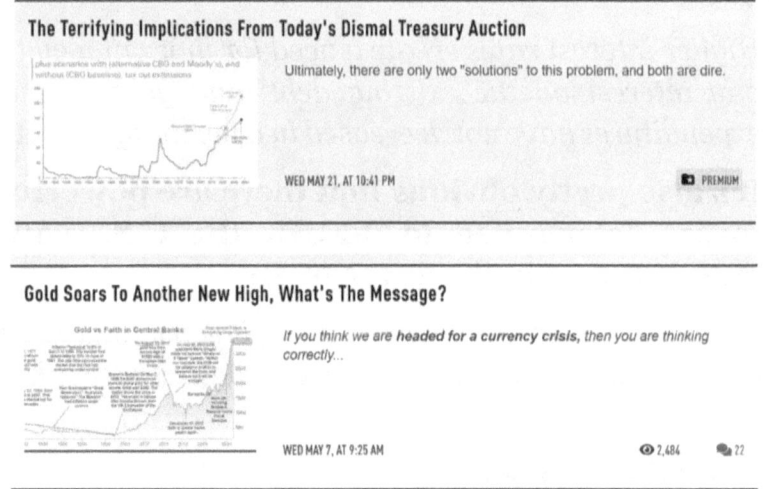

The U.S. government is still adding over $6 billion to our debt every day, and still dropping bombs on other countries.

All having non-loving intentions will get non-loving results.

I pray for peace.

Allowing it heals your mind, which projects it. A healed mind is a projection, and a protection.

Edgar Cayce

Can I please speak with Edgar Cayce?
I am always around, and hearing what you are saying in your mind because I am a guide and instructor of yours.

That's what I was going to ask you, because my spirit channel friend, William, told me that a few weeks ago.
All I can help heal in your mind, I will, because healing in your mind is all you can do while living on the Earth—meaning it is all a person can hope to achieve in their lifetime.

That brings me to the big topic that I would like to clarify. Different angels and beings have said that we are now in the End Times for humanity. We have each had a Life Preview before being born, and chose this particular timeline to be alive on the Earth—so, it is something that we know in our souls.
All heals in your life, or on losing it—so it has an end time in all cases, in all lives, and in every timeline.
I had many life 'end times' in my incarnations.

We are in a time now where our energy and financial systems are unsustainable, and the other systems are all broken—political, medical, educational, etc. The spirit of the Earth says it cannot sustain us much longer,

without the damage being too much to overcome. It is moving the Noth Pole to disable satellite communications in 7 more years.
Allowing it to halt militaries and commercial fishing in almost 8 years is its first goal.
It has another goal in its repositioning of the poles, and it is to end the current human era—not to harm humans, but for its own survival.
It has been in the initiation phase for 34 years now. How can a planet have billions of people on it, with needs it cannot provide for? It cannot.

The Earth's population has quadrupled since your death in 1945, after doubling in your lifetime.
And each person has needs that are exponentially greater now.

Humans used to live in harmony with the Earth, and had done so for thousands of years.
That ended in the modern era, having all forms of communication which has had a negative effect on people's minds.

You must know my thoughts on that—watching television is like having an open sewer in the house.
I do, and it is almost analogous in its meaning—except a sewer has excrement that can be cleaned, and eliminated from your house.

It is exponentially worse now because it's not just a TV in the house, it's on everyone's phone.

Throw in social media platforms, brainwashing engines...
And how can everyone being dissatisfied be in the best interest of the Earth? It cannot, and is another unsustainable system in life that you had mentioned.

I used to make predictions, but now I believe that we create our own individual universes, and our own futures every moment, in our minds.
I am infinite consciousness, and I will die when I am ready to die. I don't care about future predictions. That being said...
I can agree in having a lifetime that is not worried about the future, but having a lifetime backup plan is not being afraid—it is being prepared.
I can give you helpful ideas on how I would prepare.

Awesome—I was about to ask.
I would have at least 18 days of food on hand for your family—including enough fresh water for 1 month, or more.

How about having a solar powered water distiller?
I like it if it can produce enough water for a family each day.

Please continue with the preparedness items, then we'll get to the predictions for the future.
Allowing for almost no money exchanging means you will need something that can be used for exchange.

How about silver... or fresh water?

In a collapsing society, silver will not be very useful if you cannot eat it. I would have a lot of freeze-dried food, and a lot of land to plant seeds, in a hidden location.

What else will I need in the not-so-distant future?
You will need like-minded people, having the same goals as yourself—with complementary abilities—with a lot of energy, and a lot of determination to survive.

Is that everything?
You could have chicken for eggs, and a lot of chicken feed for the winter months. Having firewood for heating is also important.
I can give you a lot of advice on how I would acclimate without food for extended periods. Make a lot of food that can be dried and eaten later, such as all kinds of cookies with protein in them. I meant, to have them freeze-dried for better longevity. How else can I be of help to you?

Can you please give me a bullet point outline of upcoming events in chronological order? I understand that some events are planned or fabricated, and others will be natural.
All of them are in a state of flux, meaning almost in order, but not entirely. Each event could also not even happen as we are discussing—but it could, making it a highly likely event.

How many impactful events or changes should I expect in the next 5 years?
All are about having less money, and a lot fewer liberties in life—although how could liberties be taken away if half of the electorate does not want them?
All have been in a large development stage for many years. All of them are designed for controlling people, and allowing controllers more tyrannical surveillance in allowing controllers total access to peoples' thoughts.

How many items will I be listing?
Four big ones, and 6 smaller ones.

Okay, let's hear it.
All have a number, and a letter for its minor amendments.

Number 1 has 1 amendment.

All having an account in a bank having any money in it will be digitized. All of it will be a lot less in terms of value.

Here is the amendment (a). Will people continue to use the banks? All having a need for transactions in larger amounts will have to have an account for them.

How can it be allowed if half of the people do not want it? An awful lot of people do want it, and have no need for physical money, they think.

Number 2 has 2 amendments to it.

All having an account in a bank will have a digital I.D. that accesses all of their information in their digital devices.

(a) How could a lot of people want their digital information shared? It is being accessed now in many instances.

(b) How can it be accessed now with no objections? People have a belief in its confidentiality, and that it is necessary.

Number 3 has no amendments to it.

A digital I.D. will have your retinal scan and DNA folder in it.

Number 4 has 3 amendments to it.

A currency collapse will make all money that is not digital, worthless.

(a) How could a currency collapse and there still be a functioning government? It has digital transactions now, in all of its wasteful spending.

(b) How could a currency collapse, and all people continue in their lives? Most having no other money, will die in their despair.

(c) How could a government have this planned for its people? It has not had good intentions for 3 generations.

Central Bank Digital Currencies (CBDCs) – Accelerating towards Dystopia

by BullionStar - Friday, Sep 06, 2024 - 5:16

… globally coordinated plan to roll out retail central bank **digital** currencies (CBDCs). Billed by central banks and … involved in, or exploring, the rollout of a central bank **digital currency**. Four years ago in 2020, there were only 35 …

Crypto
Swiss City Of Lugano Embraces Diverse Digital Currency Future

by Tyler Durden - Friday, Feb 02, 2024 - 3:30

… A future where Bitcoin, stablecoins and central bank **digital** currencies can coexist in the Swiss city of Lugano is … of Lugano, is optimistic about a future where different **digital** currencies and assets could be used all together. … while retail CBDCs are seen as the standard **digital currency** for everyday payments or peer-to-peer transactions, …

Crypto
Trump Vows To "Never Allow" A Central Bank Digital Currency

by Tyler Durden - Thursday, Jan 18, 2024 - 6:11

… Wednesday vowed to never allow the use of a Central Bank **Digital Currency** (CBDC), as it would "give the government absolute … Trump says he will prevent implementation of Central Bank **Digital** Currencies (CBDC) pic.twitter.com/vheJDn2HBg — …

Crypto
Why Central Bank Digital Currencies Are Unnecessary And Dangerous

by Tyler Durden - Sunday, Feb 25, 2024 - 14:00

… have been deliberating on the concept of introducing a **digital currency**. However, many citizens fail to grasp the rationale … carried out electronically. Nevertheless, a central bank **digital currency** is much more than electronic money. I will …

Personal Finance
Hidden Agendas: Beware Of The Government's Push For A Digital Currency

by Tyler Durden - Wednesday, Sep 25, 2024 - 12:45

… agents to seize Americans' bank accounts. Make way for the **digital** dollar. Whether it's the central bank **digital currency** favored by President Biden , or the cryptocurrency …

Crypto
On The Brink Of A Dramatic Change: The Digitalization Of Money

by Tyler Durden - Thursday, Mar 28, 2024 - 20:45

… via Bitcoin Magazine, The current state of Central Bank **Digital Currency** Projects globally summarized by Efrat Enigson. … And the new one is what we call blockchain . It means **digital**. It means having an almost perfect record of every …

MICHELLE L.

I get that I knew Michelle L. "a little bit" in another lifetime. Did I?
Once, in another galaxy, in Andromeda. Although her gender was not female or male, her light being incarnation had information that would be a lifeline, actually helping you incarnate on the Earth now.

What kind of information?
It helped you in your choice of a lifetime in the ending of the human era.

Do you mean in choosing my lifetime now, from our future lifetime in Andromeda?
Yes, in choosing to incarnate in the future's past.

Is Michelle a guide of mine?
A Lightwalker like yourself, meaning a healer of immense ability.

Is that her purpose?
Her incarnation in the Earth's End Times has only one purpose—allowing herself an instance of fear, healing what it represents—nothing.

Please tell me about the "End Times."
All having an illusory existence in the Mind of God will have its end time in its last incarnation in humanity's ending.
Is humanity ending, I hear you ask? It has to end by not having any more beginnings.

It is having no more beginnings because it has been decided in the collective dream in God Mind that it is not willing for itself to continue any longer.

Why not?
A dream having no ending cannot be healing unless there is awakening. All will have an individual awakening, but to awaken in the dream means to no longer be dreaming. A dream cannot be healing for all unless all are awakened.

All awakening means having the illusory existence in the dream end—willingly for most, and unwillingly for others.

What do you mean?
Most allow a lifetime ending because it is not joyful for them, as it had been in most incarnations. Others are not willing to have a lifetime ending, although it is impossible not to have one.

When will all be awakened?
In another 48 years, there will no longer be humans on the Earth.

Is that because the pole shift—which has already started, and will disable satellite navigation in 7-½ years—will totally flip in 27 years, and cause the Earth's rotation to start reversing in 48 more years?
Yes, it allows for a new era devoid of humans in a long, colder period of Earth purification.

Can you please tell me Michelle's most interesting lifetime on the Earth?

Her most interesting lifetime had been as a lowly worker in lower-class India in the 18th century, when it was not British.
All of her healing ability was attributed to another, known as a guru. All that she looked at would heal instantaneously.
Her family had instantly healed after she was born, allowing them access in one of the guru's circles.

Does Michelle's light being self, in Andromeda in our future, have a message for her?

Her Lightwalker self has healed in your presence, and you in hers. Her lifetime incarnation on the Earth has healing herself as her goal, but it heals all who are in her presence.

Does she heal with her eyes, her hands, or mainly her presence?

Her healing has always been from her presence, allowing others a moment of absorbing her high vibration.
Her energy field is mostly bluish-green in color.

Angel Death

Is there an angel of death?
I am the Angel of Death, as you call it—although death is an illusion.

Is death an illusion, or is the dream of life an illusion?
All dreams are illusions, making all waking up in them 'having no illusions'.
Death is having no more illusions, or not having to be in the dream anymore—meaning all death can ever be is an illusion also.

What is your name?
I am Angel Death, although having that name is a misnomer—I am alive, not having experienced death.

What do you want to tell me about death?
It is a welcome event, I can assure you. No one has been dissatisfied yet, except for those who don't know they are dead.

All who have died were alive at one time, believing they were, (a) not going to die in their lifetime, if that makes any sense, or (b) living until they die, which has to make sense—although it will be a death that leaves them with no illusions in either case.

Here's my question to Angel Death—do you expect mass death in the United States in our upcoming future?

I do—accelerating in the near future, and culminating in the not-too-distant future.

Please explain.
There will be mass death in the United States in 4 years when its currency has no more value in its collapsing.
All I can do is alert you to mass deaths, nothing else.

How do you know about it?
I am Angel Death—I know all about it.

How much mass death will there be in the United States, and when?
In about 4 more years, a currency collapse will leave most Americans without food or clean water—80% will have no means of acquiring either of them, and have no alternative to death.

What percentage of Americans will die in the next 5 years?
The majority will die in the last year in your time frame, and it will be about 40%.

I believe that death is a welcome event, but how can I avoid it if everyone else is doing it? I like going against the crowd.
Go headlong into your plans to move to West Virginia. It is going to be a safe haven for you and others.

When should I move there?
In about 5 months would be death incompatible, although it could be up to 1 year.

I like your term "death incompatible."

All in life can be "death incompatible" if you affirm it like this—"All in my life, and all in my death are not compatible as long as I am living—which is as long as I wish."

I like it.
Affirm it, and be compatible with life by loving it.

You mentioned a U.S. currency collapse in 4 years, which matches what Edgar Cayce and other spirits have told me.
How certain is that to happen, and at that time?
I can comment on the death component, which will be a collapse also—in terms of living people in the United States.

Is there a time when most people who are now living in the United States will have died?
In 8-1/2 more years, they will mostly have died.

From what?
Dehydration is number one, then getting killed by another person is second, and having no food is third.

What is fourth?... just for giggles.
Fourth is lack of hope, meaning death from despair.

Thank you, Angel Death.
I am Angel Death, and I bid you so long, for now.

Admiral Richard Byrd

Can I speak with Admiral Richard E. Byrd?
Admiral Byrd, as I was known, has a lot I can communicate to you.

Please tell me.
I can answer all of the questions I hear in your mind, although I am in another dimension—not having a body in a physical sense, but I have one in an energetic dimension that has no limits.

I can describe what I'm doing as having had a dream of my life, and I have come to heal all I had done, and all I did not have the courage to do while I was alive. All I could have done was to be more honest by not concealing my discovery.

Not allowing myself to discuss it had made it harder for my heart.

If I could have made it known where the inner-earth entrance is, there could have been more decisions on how atomic bombs do not benefit humanity. Having allowed myself to discuss the inner-earth would have had an enormous impact on humanity.

Humanity has total disregard for the planet, in my opinion.

Inside the Earth is a civilization that can control the magnetic poles. In a geomagnetic reversal, it is the ending of each era.

Humanity is nearing the ending of its current era. How could it not end in the near future, because the Earth cannot sustain humans much longer.

How much longer does humanity have?
Humanity has 8 more years, or less, before the poles move enough in repositioning to disable satellite navigation.

This eliminates commercial fishing, which is destroying the underwater ecology of the planet. It also disables all navigational systems which enable all military operations that are also an ecological disaster for the planet.

A message I received while writing, *Mysteries, Prophecies, and the Hollow Earth* said that you had located the entrance to the inner-earth in one of your early expeditions to Antarctica. You flew down 4,000 feet below the Earth's surface, and saw the hanging pods of inner-earth beings, and declared that they were bird nests. You became very nervous because your compass stopped working at that level, and you returned to the surface. Pictures at that time often show you holding your compass.
I had allowed myself to only go down to the inner-earth entrance, but I could have gone into it if I had more courage. I have always had a regret about not doing that.

Can you tell me if space images of the Earth have 'whited out' the entrance to the inner-earth in Antarctica?

It has, and it is closely held information that remains secret.

That implies that countries like Russia, China, and the U.S. are all working together to keep it a secret.
It is not allowed to be public information, because all beliefs that people hold onto would be destroyed.

Still, the bigger picture is that the world controllers work together, but appear to be adversaries to keep everyone off balance, afraid, and under control.
All control means is having more power for themselves, and none for anyone else on the Earth– including inside the Earth.

My last topic is the ending of the human era. When is it?
It has begun in its final ending phases which are:
- *allowing and increasing social decay and financial ruin for everyone.*
- *halting all of the information from the inner-earth from ever being revealed.*
- *increasing military activity and fear on the Earth's surface*
- *and having the internet become a weapon for people to destroy themselves with.*

What do you mean?
All control is having information to influence behavior. In another few years, it will all be on the

internet, and under central control—meaning it can, and will be used to influence everyone's behavior.

What will happen?
Controllers have been preparing a safe haven for themselves on Maui, and have decided that all others on the planet will no longer be necessary, and can be eliminated. In about 4 more years, all of their central control of information—including all money—will be deleted from everyone's accounts.

Lovely.
It begins an almost hellish world of people killing, and being killed for food and water.

It's the end game for humanity.
It has been deemed an end game for humanity, and a new era for the Earth.

Do the controllers know about the geomagnetic repositioning, and the upcoming pole reversal?
They already have another navigation system that uses the stars, and not a magnetic North Pole for direction.

Do they know that the poles will flip in about 27 more years, causing cataclysms and eventually the Earth's rotation to reverse?
They do not know all of the future history, no.

Thank you, Admiral Byrd.
I can give you advice in your endeavor to live safely into a future having little, or no social cohesion.

You have already decided to live in a West Virginia town, near where you are now. I had lived in that vicinity in my earlier years.

I recommend for you—although it may not be important now—to have a large supply of dehydrated food that can be hydrated and eaten, in a future with little or no food in some months.

What kind of dehydrated foods?
All having a lot of protein in it, such as egg whites, and even dried milk has a lot of protein.

I could store seeds from pumpkins, flax, and sunflowers—plus nuts. I could also stockpile beans to cook in water over a wood fire.
All having a long shelf life, if stored properly.

Lulo
The Inner-Earth

I'd like to discuss the inner-earth. Here are highlights from my 2023 book, *Mysteries, Prophecies, and the Hollow Earth*.

- the Earth has an average 80-mile thick crust, and a honeycombed interior, with several entrance locations. The largest is in Antarctica, and is whited-out on satellite images
- numerous political and religious leaders visit Antarctica regularly
- there are inhabitants in the inner-earth under southern Australia, whose ancestors had come to Earth from Mars 319,000 years ago
- they left Mars because they knew that their atmosphere of helium would be destroyed by a solar flare
- there are 3 types of beings in the inner-earth: light beings, human-type beings, and animal-human hybrids.
- the animal-human hybrids are depicted in Egyptian murals and statues
- the Mars beings "light-constructed" the pyramids in Egypt and Mexico to moor their spacecraft.
- they traversed dimensions to arrive here in cigar-shaped crafts that are 1/2 mile long. They had 19 of them in that millennium

- they did not find the Earth suitable for them to inhabit, with too little helium to breathe
- they continued on to the Constellation Taurus and settled there
- some stayed behind as settlers and hibernated in the inner-earth, as they altered their DNA to breathe oxygen/nitrogen
- they have light machine technology in the inner-earth, where the physics is reversed
- the inner-earth was called the Garden of Eden in the Bible, and the plant life there is luminous
- a group of inner-earth beings came to the surface, led by Adam and Eve—whose original names are Hadim and Ebelon
- Hadim and Ebelon were chosen to lead because they made intelligent decisions, allowing the group to survive
- in 1939, Admiral Byrd flew down into the inner-earth entrance, and became highly nervous when his compass stopped working below -4000 feet
- he saw hanging pod structures at the entrance, and declared that they were bird nests. He was instructed by military commanders to never mention it again
- our detonation of atomic bombs in 1945 prompted the inner-earth beings into action to depopulate the Earth of humans on the surface
- they are not supposed to interfere with the course of humanity, but say it is helping more than

hurting, and is necessary for their survival, and that of the Earth
- they say that the Earth and oceans cannot sustain themselves much longer at the current rate of destruction
- the inner-earth beings are moving the magnetic North Pole with their light machine technology, and the energy creates crop circles
- the North Pole is moving fast, and will have moved 80 degrees in 7-8 more years to disable satellite navigation
- loss of satellite navigation will achieve their first goal of halting militaries and commercial fishing
- light beings from the inner-earth have permanently disabled our intercontinental nuclear missiles, as reported by military leaders numerous times
- in 27 years, a geomagnetic reversal, or pole shift will mark the end of the human era
- in about 47 years, the Earth will start to rotate in the opposite direction and start a new era devoid of humans
- cataclysms on the Earth's surface will cause some continents to be submerged under the oceans, and some ocean floor areas will become land areas

Here is additional 2024 information about the inner-earth, published in my book, *The 4 Secrets of the Universe*, from May 2024.

Lulo
Intrusions into the Inner Earth

What will be on the Earth in 1,000 years?
Humans have terminated their species, illogically.
All of the hopeless intrusions into the inner-earth have been halted, and Earth has a much lower interior and exterior temperature.
Halting all human activity allows the ocean fish that humanity has depleted, to recover.
All human actions that have harmed the Earth cease in their operations.
A hologram has light in its center, making its holographic illumination alternate in God Mind, with no hatred on the Earth.

What are the "*hopeless intrusions into the inner-earth*"?
A military intrusion by the almost impossibly arrogant and aggressive actors halting love on the planet.

Has the U.S. invaded the inner-earth?
An expedition has entered the inner-earth, against the inner-earth beings' wishes.

When did they enter?
About 2 years ago.

Can inner-earth beings or light beings repel them?
Allowing them to enter makes their hatred of inner-earth beings less intense.

Why do they hate inner-earth beings?
All beings that have animalistic features are hated in their minds.

Has the intrusion, along with accelerated depletion of the Earth's resources, prompted the inner-earth beings to shift the Earth's magnetic north pole more rapidly with their light machine?
Ending all military and commercial fishing activities in their loss of satellite communications, yes.

The Earth is hollow, correct?
The Earth is hollow, and has a honeycombed interior.

Beings originally from Mars inhabit the inner-earth. They were pioneers that hibernated after staying behind from the Mars group that was looking for another planet to inhabit, knowing that the Mars' atmosphere would be destroyed by a massive solar flare.
Adam and Eve were in that group, and the Garden of Eden is the inner-earth, where plant life is luminous.
All that is in your account is correct.

Now, 2 months later on 6-30-24, I'd like to get an update from the inner-earth.
A larger expedition has entered the inner-earth in the last 8 weeks, making all of the inner-earth beings lives in danger.
Aggressive and arrogant actors have decided all inner-earth beings should be eliminated in their hatefulness.

Extermination of the inner-earth beings will not be allowed. Attempting to exterminate inner-earth beings illogically causes the demise of the invading force, and not our extermination.

Will you neutralize the invaders in self-defense?
All must defend themselves from non-love in the inner-earth.

Go for it. How will you stop them?
A frequency emission that halts a heart from circulating blood will be deployed as a defensive mechanism.

How are plans coming along to shift the magnetic North Pole, disabling satellite navigation—and putting a halt to militaries and commercial fishing operations?
Halting all military operations and commercial fishing has been a goal of the Earth itself, not just inner-earth beings.
Our being directed by the Earth's spirit is not interfering with the planet. A geomagnetic reversal is going to happen if we accelerate it or not, allowing the Earth to heal itself in time—meaning heal itself after humans are gone from the planet.

Is the magnetic North Pole moving rapidly?
Allowing the Earth to impair the functioning of satellites in about 8 more years—a decision that cannot be reversed without the Earth asking for it to be delayed. All of the destructive activities continue,

and the Earth has little going for it without the ending of the human era.

New Update: March 2025

An inner-earth leader named Lulo has this to say—
"Hello informed one on the surface. I have discussed my role with you before.
I am Lulo, and am communicating from all in the inner-earth, now in March 2025, from one mind. All in the inner-earth have been held by an invasion force from the surface, that has malicious intentions. All I can do is let them know in their minds that I can terminate them in a few seconds, without them having time to respond. I am afraid they will have more intruders to come and kill us. I am allowing healing in their minds because I do not kill intentionally without provocation."

Do whatever you have to do to protect yourselves. If they die, then that is their lifetime ending chosen by them. We create our own realities.

Can you prevent more intrusions into the inner-earth by using your light technology to disable their surface base in Antarctica, or to block their entry point?

I can do all of those interventions to protect us, if I can have your permission for taking action steps.

My permission? If you can stop the intruders' hearts, could you do something else like disable their bowel control? That would certainly be debilitating.
I can alter all of their bodily functions with my mind, without killing them.

I am thinking that you can also paralyze their arms. That would certainly disable them. They will call it 'Inner-Earth Disease' and be afraid to return.

You could also disable their weapons, like you did to the nuclear warheads on the surface.
I am allowing myself to initiate actions you have suggested, and have the approval of all in the inner-earth.

When you disable one of the intruders, it will take two more to remove him to the surface—so you can do one at a time. How many are there?
About 18 or 19—they come and go.

I will check back with you often.
All here are in agreement on disabling their bowels and their weapons.

That should be interesting.
Allowing the arrogant actors to leave will be a welcome event.

It will be hard to be arrogant with no bowel control, and paralyzed arms.

I am in agreement with it, although you find it comical.

LULO
CIVILIZATION INSIDE THE EARTH

[One day later]

Lulo, you are in a dangerous situation there. What is happening today?
The inexplicable loss of arm movement and bowel control has disabled one of the intruding army people. Another one is helping him, and considering leaving there.

I'd like to get more details. Do the intruders wear space suits or breathing apparatus?
They all have on a garment having an air chamber that they can get air from.

Do they have some kind of vehicles, or did they walk into the inner-earth where you are?
It would be impossible to drive into the inner-earth. they all made the trek on foot.

How far is it from the entrance to where you are, in Earth miles?
About 800 miles in a straight line, but there are a lot of obstacles to navigate around—making it a lot longer in distance, and in the time it takes to get here.

Did the invaders bring food?
Enough for several months, yes.

And water?
There is enough in the inner-earth for them to capture and drink.

Are they able to navigate to find their way out?
In having survival skills, they left markers on their trail.

How many days does it take for them to return to the surface, when knowing the way?
About 40 days is the average amount of time it would take.

Can they communicate with others on the surface?
Having no power or communications in the inner-earth, they cannot.

Are Earth leaders on the surface aware of the inner-earth beings?
Eight have direct knowledge, and about 50 have indirect knowledge of our civilization inside the Earth.

Do you think it would be a good idea for about half of the intruders to become disabled with Bowel-Arm Disorder (BAD), so that they will all decide to leave, and be afraid to return?
We agree that it will have the intended effect on the intruders.

Maybe the other half should become afflicted as they return to their surface base, then have it wear off in a couple of weeks.
Having all of them feel the effects will deter them from ever coming into the inner-earth again.

Can you influence their minds, such as erasing their memories of having made contact with inner-earth beings?
I cannot do that, but I can have a light being do it.

That is something you can have done to the intruders as they return to the surface.
I can have it done as each one comes to the surface. All in the inner-earth agree with your guidance.

I want all beings to live peacefully—happy and free.
All here are in agreement, wishing you the same in your life, and in all of your lifetimes.

Thank you, Lulo. I will check back with you again—and will pray for your safety, and for the success of our plan to rid the inner-earth of invaders.
I am grateful for your helpful suggestions and prayers. Please help us with your knowledge of the Merkabah.

Lulo
A Merkabah

I detailed the Merkabah in my books, *The Book of Manifesting* and *The 4 Secrets of the Universe*.

Here is the summary from pages 37-38 of *The 4 Secrets of the Universe*:

A Merkabah is a flowing, healing, light-activator.

A Merkabah has healed God Mind illumination all around it and inside of it.

A healed God Mind illumination manifests in life.

All Merkabah energy has life-mind knowledge illuminating healed all around it and inside of it—healed in God Mind.

Imagine being healed, illuminating inside of one.

God Mind healing halts non-love, activating life-mind healing... healing the mind in about a minute.

A Merkabah illuminates God Mind in your mind, allowing healing illumination.

All illuminating in the Frequency of God Mind (405nm light) and in a Merkabah, circle in a feedback loop into God Mind healed, and into the Light Mind healed.

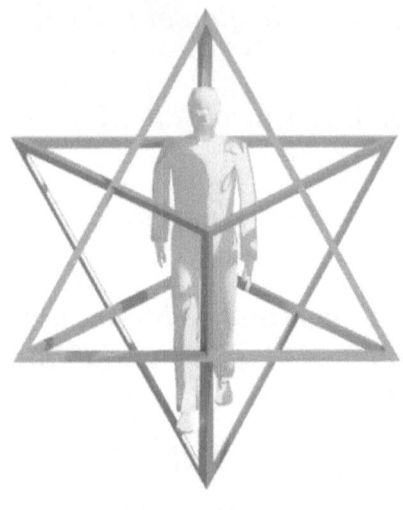

A Merkabah, artwork by Ryan Classen.

HEALED IN GOD MIND INSTANTLY[5]

To God Mind—Please correct or add to my instructions for someone to use the Merkabah.

1. Picture yourself inside of the Merkabah looking out.

Acclimating higher or lower to fit inside of it.

2. Activate it by visualizing the God Mind frequency of 405nm blue light all around and inside of it.

Activate it by illuminating it, making the illumination increase in intensity to God Mind infinite lightness.

3. Program the Merkabah with your wishes for things that are good.

---

[5] From *The 4 Secrets of the Universe.*

And hold the almost healed desires in the Merkabah's center, near the heart.

Love the desire healing in God Mind.

4. Notice the healed desires effortlessly manifesting in reality.
Allow healed desires illumination in the hologram of life.

Is that everything?
All healed in God Mind is everything, so yes.

What about the breath?
Allow breaths to inhale on your wish, and exhale on it healing.

Lulo, do you understand it?
I acclimated in your mind having read it again, and understand.

I just read these chapters for you from *The 4 Secrets of the Universe*:
- The Most Powerful Manifesting Engine
- Programming of a Loving Intention
- Illumination of Your Desires
- Healed in God Mind Instantly
- The Earth Merkabah

Acclimating it in my mind has implications of worldwide impact. It can heal the whole world, and is happening as we communicate.

Is there still a human depopulation agenda for those on the Earth's surface?
Humans have overly depleted the Earth's resources, and have no intentions for discontinuing the destruction.

All having had injections to modify their DNA are not likely to live long lifespans.

Will the world population continue to shrink?
Cancer and infertility will make the human population shrink continuously, and collapse in a geomagnetic reversal in about 27 more years.

That's what I was getting at—are we near the ending of the human era?
All eras end in a geomagnetic reversal, meaning, yes—because the geomagnetic reversal has started, and will become inverted in the next 27 or 28 more years, causing cataclysms that humans cannot survive in their fragile state.

In its aftermath, the Earth can renew itself in an era without humans. After an era without humans, there will be an era having highly advanced humans that love themselves, and love the Earth.

Will you and the inner-earth beings survive the geomagnetic reversal?
In the inner-earth, we will not have adverse effects other than hearing a lot of upheaval of continents and ocean areas.

The Earth has a light holographic center that we can control, and cause the Earth's poles to shift.

It cannot be delayed, unless the Earth asks for it to be delayed.

That is discussed in my book, *Mysteries, Prophecies, and the Hollow Earth*.
It has a lot of information that you can reference for your readers.

Thank you, Lulo.
All in the inner-earth thank you for communicating to us how to heal in a Merkabah.

You are welcome. I will check back with you in a few days.
I am healing myself in a Merkabah, and will communicate with you then.

Lulo
Return to the Surface

[2 days later, February 14, 2025]

Lulo, Can you please give me an update?
All I can report is that another invader has become incontinent, and his arms are paralyzed.
Another one is helping him, and is considering for all of them to return to the surface.

Good. Do you know if they have any intentions to harm or kill any inner-earth beings?
All of them have incredibly heinous thoughts, but have declared that harming any inner-earth beings would not be allowed.

Do not hesitate to use deadly force to defend yourselves if they do. That's the way it works on the surface.
I cannot use deadly force without deadly intentions. In my mind, it makes me a killer.
Making myself a killer is less desirable than having myself be killed.

You can use our current disabling method, but let's expect they will decide to leave.
It appears they have decided on leaving in about 4 hours.

I'd make the Bowel-Arm Disorder intermittent so they can make better progress returning to the surface—then have more of them become afflicted temporarily as they get closer, and when they return to their base.
Then erase their memories of their inner-earth experiences.
I am in agreement with your plan for them to forget about it, and to have no interest in the inner-earth, other than, "Forget about it."

How long will it take them to get to the surface?
About 18 days is the fastest they could make it to a surface opening, nearer to where we are.
It would take many more days to return to the surface where they entered from.

Good luck. I will check back with you again.
I am grateful for your guidance, as all in the inner-earth have been.

I know you are about 800 miles from the Antarctica entrance, but how deep below the Earth's surface are you?
About 80 miles thick is the Earth's crust, and where we live is on the inner crust.

Lulo
Ala

[12 days later, Feb. 26, 2025]

Can I speak with Lulo please?
I am here, and hearing your words.

I am checking back in with the inner-earth. Are you all safe?
All of the inner-earth beings are happy that the invasion force had decided to return to the surface.
In your time, it was 3-1/2 days ago.

I trust that they will make their way back to their base in Antarctica, recover from (BAD), and have all memories and photos of their adventure wiped clean—and they will vow never to return to the inner-earth.
I can acknowledge that that will be the most advantageous outcome for everyone in the inner-earth, and in the invasion force. All in the inner-earth have a lot of appreciation for your guidance.
It gave the invaders a reason to leave, and no one was harmed.

Now that that is taken care of, do you need anything else?
I can grant all that you wish for in your mind.

WHAT?!
A light being can grant all that you wish for in your mind.

You said "all," and we have an expression here that is, 'be careful what you wish for'.
All I can wish for is peace and well-being for humankind, and the inner-earth beings I call my family.

I wish for that too, plus having a healed mind. A healed mind can manifest its desires.
I explained it in *The Book of Manifesting*.
I know how you allow healing your mind to be a priority over other worldly desires.

Is there a particular light being that will grant my wishes?
I am having one of our highest light beings named 'Ala' come into your world, and heal your mind.
Ala can hear your calls for assistance now, and into your future.

Thank you very much, Lulo and Ala. I look forward to healing in this lifetime, because it will heal all of my lifetimes and incarnations. I wrote about that in *The 4 Secrets of the Universe*.
I can also have your books more widely accepted.

Thank you for that. Speaking of *The 4 Secrets* and this book *The 5th Secret*, is there a 6th Secret of the Universe? It could be the topic for the next book.

Here it is, and it is you. When you heal your mind, there is no more universe as you knew it.

All there is is yourself that is healed. How can anything unhealed exist in your healed mind? It can't. It can only be God yourself being all that can ever be, which is all that there is.

That is very profound. I have to let all of this sink in.

Thank you, Lulo and Ala, and all of the guests in the spirit world who contributed to my exploration of consciousness in these chapters.

I have more to say. Ala has a message for you to hear.

"I am Ala, a light being from the inner-earth where I have been for millions of years, in your terms—but only as a light being where I am infinite.

How can I be infinite in a finite world?—because 'infinite' is inside of yourself, and 'finite' is outside of yourself.

Do not concern yourself with finite matters in the world. Infinity inside of yourself is all that matters, where I am in your light that has God as its source. I am infinite light, as well as God, and also yourself.

Ala has nothing more I can do besides healing your mind, which illuminates healed in God Mind.

Healed in God Mind is all there can be."

Thank you, Ala.

I hear what is being asked in your mind. I am 'Ala', illuminating in the Mind of God.
The Islamic word for God is 'Allah', which is also the name for God yourself.

"Allah" is God in each of us.
"Allah" is all there is, so it is the healed illumination in all of life, including my light which is called 'Ala'.

You are healed light, which is God. God is the source of healed light, and I have some healed light, as well as everyone else.
Allah is all there is, and God is Allah. Illuminate all there is, and you illuminate all there is from your healed mind which allows itself to heal.

Thank you, Ala. Let's heal—I allow it.
I am healed, and am healing all you allow me to. All having a need to heal is not your concern anymore.

I am healed. Ala has healed my mind.
I had healed all that needed healing, which no longer has meaning for you.

It had served its purpose, and only existed in my mind.
It had meaning, and served its purpose—and has healed and disappeared, along with its meaning.

What has meaning in my life now?
All that has meaning is God's illumination of your mind, making you one with God.
All other godless illusions no longer have meaning in your life.

So, they will not have a purpose, and will not affect my life?
They no longer exist in your healed mind that illuminates a projection of a universe for you to experience yourself in, yes.

I would like that to be the 'take away' for readers of this book.
A book can heal all that allow their minds to heal. How can it have any other purpose? Nothing has a purpose that cannot be healed.

Ala, would you like to give any closing statements to readers?
I am Ala, illuminating from the Mind of God. I will illuminate in your mind from here to infinity, if you allow me to.

I like that term, "from here to infinity."
Infinity is never ending. Only what you give meaning to has an ending.

I, and readers of this book, will heal from here to infinity.
You are here now, infinitely healed.

That's the 5th Secret—"Here I am."
And here I am—infinite light that is healed in the Mind of God yourself, from here to infinity.

Robert

With whom can I speak now?
I am an old friend, and have not died, but am communicating with you from my spirit.
I am Robert from high school, and our days before and after that. I have a healing request to make, please.
I am about to have an operation for cancer in my lungs. I do not expect it to heal—I have chosen it to leave altogether, having no other options at this point.

We were best friends for a really long time.
Actually, in our soul groups, we are still best friends, and I can hear what you want to say.
All has been a personal loss to you in this lifetime, it sounds like. All has been a spiritual gain in losing the attachments.
All has been a dream where God is dreaming it can be separate beings—not only having love, but non-love that has to heal.

What would you like to heal?
Please forgive me for having envy in my mind that I could not heal.

I forgive you.
I am healed for having envy, and you are healed for forgiving me.

I think you only need to forgive yourself to heal both you and me. It heals me for accepting your forgiveness.
I know, and can now forgive myself by having your forgiveness in advance.

Is your lifespan almost completed?
It has beginning and ending dates that are almost the same, but 66 years apart.

Your birthday is in 6 months.
Allowing myself a cancer has been a blessing, allowing me to be closer to my kids than ever before.

It's great to talk to you Robert, after so long.
I had to hear in my mind that you forgave me.

Abundance

Who will I communicate with next?
I am an energy being, having nothing to identify myself with besides Abundance.

Are you a being?
I am, and always have abundance I can offer to all who hear and accept me in their hearts and minds.

That's interesting. I will volunteer. I am curious—please tell me how that works.
Affirm me by hearing this, and accepting me into your heart—"I am allowing Abundance in my life, and it emanates from my heart where it lives."

Thank you. Will you be in my heart?
I am in your heart, because your mind allowed me by affirming my mantra.
How will it make my life better?—you are asking in your mind. I am a being having only abundance, and I am emanating from your heart—not 'in' your heart, but 'from' your heart—meaning I am all around your heart, but not in it. Not being in your heart makes your heart's desires not the same as mine.
I can emanate abundance, having only your heart's desires become healed manifestations in your life.

That would be wonderful.
I am Abundance, and have healed your heart's desires for all goodness, all peacefulness, and all healthfulness.

I am energizing your financial prosperity, and your book publishing readership to both increase greatly.

Thank you very much Abundance. Is that your name?
I am also called "God"—or your loving thoughts which have infinite and eternal life in me—not 'in' me, 'as' me—having healed them in you.

At the beginning, you said you are "*a being.*"
'In' and 'as' you, yes. I am healed, meaning I cannot be not healed. All not being healed is an illusion.

Can readers of this book emanate abundance by affirming your mantra for allowing abundance?
All hearing or having read this, and affirming my mantra, will emanate abundance from their hearts. Emanating abundance will heal their hearts' desires, allowing them to manifest in their lives.

What else can you tell me about abundance?
I am all goodness and peacefulness, making all goodness and peacefulness your Godliness.
Your Godliness can manifest its desires. How can I not?

My Godliness doesn't want or need anything— just to be its own goodness and peacefulness.
Affirming this heals in your mind: "I am God having all desires of goodness and peacefulness heal my life-mind, having no other desires.
My healed life-mind manifests its desires of goodness and peacefulness."

"I am God, and manifest my heart's desires of goodness and peacefulness. How could I not?"
Affirming it heals it, making it your reality.

Thank you, Abundance! I look forward to manifesting goodness and peacefulness—with you as my Godliness.
'In' and 'as' my Godliness will heal your life-mind, which manifests more Godliness, which heals your mind, manifesting more Godliness, and so on.

In all of my lifetimes, now and forever.
Infinitely and eternally, meaning now in the Mind of God, yes.

So be it.
"Amen," I can hear in your mind, and in my heart around yours.

JOHN S.

I am open to communicate with others I have known, or not.
Hi Paul, it is John S. here.

Hi John, I was thinking about you.
I am glad you can hear in your mind, what I have in my mind. How am I now, you are wondering?
I am as good as ever, now that I am healed in an incredible lightness, having no description in words.

I remember right after you died 20 years ago, that your messages to me were pretty angry, calling your 3 cancer doctors "murderers."
At that moment, I had not been instructed how I manifested my own agreement for leaving the planet, and my earthly life.

I assume that you were met by angels and guides, given a Life Review, and have been studying your life lessons in classrooms.
I have experienced all of them in my afterlife, meaning in a lightness world I have come into.

How are you?
I am all God has promised I could be, and I do not have a need for anything else, other than a last request from you.
Can I ask you a big favor?

Sure.

In the office building where I had my business, I had 18 Gold one-ounce coins hidden in the wall where my desk was.
I hid them a long time ago, and forgot until after I had died. Nothing has been discovered yet—I know you are wondering.

I will tell Lou, and the building must have been sold at least once since then.
Do not tell Lou. He will not be able to get into the building like you will.

I am doing drawings for a project two blocks from there—renovating the Jai Medical Center. I'll drive by your building, and see what is there now. It was a good spot for your contracting business, and my office was across the street at that time until the year 2000. You passed away in 2004, and I assume your building was sold then. Lou has relocated his own business.
Getting the Gold to my wife is the goal.

Getting into the building, and finding it is the goal.
Having it all recovered and not stolen by you is your humorous thought—that is the goal.

Ha, ha—you're right.
I had a big laugh when you came to inspect my house for environmental exposures, and you said, "You don't have to worry unless I come back wearing a space suit." I am laughing again now.

You were very sick at the time, but doing better. I had done some energetic healing for you then. There was also a high level of radon gas.
I know, and I am grateful for all you have done. How can I help you in your earthly healing?

I will leave it up to you. Do you have any suggestions—other than giving me 18 Gold coins? ☺
A book can sell a million copies if it is good, and people know about it. I can enhance it to heal a million minds in the not so distant timeline.

That would be awesome—thank you, John! Have you seen your brother Bruce who had died younger also?
I have, and he is here now wishing for all of your wishes to come true in life.

Thank you, Bruce and John!
I can hear the Gold coins jingling in your pocket now.

If you said there are 100 coins hidden, rather than 18, I'd buy the building to get access... since Gold now costs 10x more than 25 years ago.
I could arrange it, if you are going to sell a million books.

If I sell a million books, I'll buy your wife 18 Gold coins.
I can agree to that—keep on writing!

I like win-win-win solutions for everything.
All winning has healing as its purpose. All in your books heals in the minds of readers.

Chris T.

Does Chris T. want to talk to me?
How did you know? I could hear you thinking about me.

I had a lot of contractor friends die before getting old. It is a stressful occupation.
It had a lot of stressful moments that could not heal themselves very fast.

They all had piled up, and became insurmountable to heal if I kept adding to them.

You had called me from the hospital, and said that your "Crohn's was acting up."
I expected that you would be treated and released, but you died only a day or two later.
Actually, it was after 3 more days, and I did die—having no more earthly obligations to complete.

Can you tell me what happened?
All of my obligations had been only to myself—not to anyone else, except God, which is myself.
All had been completed in that lifetime, and I could hear myself saying that it was time to go home.
In the hospital, an angel came to discuss that with me. It made me want to go with it, when I learned where we were going.
After I had accepted all it had discussed with me, an illumination in my head exploded in the most intense lightness—and all I could feel was God's love all

around me and through me, healing my lifetime concerns.
A gentle pulling had me moving into the light, and out of my body through the top of my head.
I had not been more elated in my life when I was out of my body. Not having a body meant not having an ego identity anymore. I had been healed by God, not by the doctors.

Where did the angel take you?
I accepted its invitation to follow it higher and away from the Earth. I then came into a large auditorium which had a 3-dimensional movie of my life playing on a 3-dimensional screen.

I could hear and feel what everyone else in the movie heard and felt from interacting with me.
I had a lot of healing to do—of myself, not them—because they are myself.
Healing myself is all I can ever do, with that insight.
All I can ever be is God loving itself to heal, because how could God not love, and how could I not be God? It is inconceivable for either of them to be something else.
After I had heard and felt all I could have done better in life with, I made an agreement with myself to completely heal myself, meaning me and all of the others as one. Then I entered a classroom, and have been having lessons from each person in the film of my life—each person in the movie of healing myself by meeting myself.

Not allowing myself to have an instance of non-love means to always love myself, no matter how I may have acted in the past. I am always having to have that in my mind, because everything manifests instantly here.

What should I and readers of this book do, or understand while we are alive?
Act like it doesn't matter what goes on in the world, because when you're dead, it doesn't.
It only matters how it affects your ability to respond with love.

That is a very profound and important statement.
It can help you to heal what you have in your mind, not having more things to heal piled on top of it.

Nostradamus
Awareness Is a Choice

May I speak with Nostradamus?
Hello, Gorman. How can I assist you today?

Hello, Michel. I would like to talk to you about how we create our individual universes, and to thank you for teaching me how to dowse information when I worked for you in your lifetime as Nostradamus.[6]
I always had admiration for your interest in learning about how consciousness is conscious of itself.
It cannot be conscious of itself if it is not conscious awareness. Not being conscious of itself has no conscious awareness. You see, it can only be all that it is, and that is God as yourself.
I am God allowing God in my mind, which is aware that I am allowing. It cannot be unaware in its awareness.
Can a being have instructions to heal in its awareness? Only in a human mind where awareness is a choice.

Here is a poem from my book, *Sojourn*.
I love it, favoring the future self imagery.

---

[6] Explained in "A Courier of Important Messages" in *The 4 Secrets of the Universe.*

I Know – You Know

Why couldn't I
  have been born wise
infant eyes
  that could see through lies

and an infant heart
  infinitely smart
off to a good start
  and won't break apart

and infant ears
  that would only hear
the love held dear
  with nothing to fear

and hands that will hold
what feeds my soul
(whispering) I know you know, baby
as I grow old

Let's talk about that. Do we each have a future self, or just our higher selves—not necessarily in time at all?
All have higher and lower selves in their healed, and unhealed parts of their minds. Higher selves illuminate God, and lower selves do not illuminate, as they need healing.

All in the future has nothing to heal if it comes from the higher self. All coming from the lower self needs to heal.
How can it heal if it is not created first? It can heal in the mind, and it will not need to be created.

What I say is that there are malignancies in mass consciousness that need to be born, so they can die.
In "your" consciousness is more accurate wording.

In "my" consciousness? Am I not affected by mass consciousness?
All consciousness is coming from your mind is astounding in its ability to heal, making it all it can be—and correcting itself for you to be all you can be.

If I raise my consciousness, does it change my entire universe?
It can only be a projection of what you need to heal in.

If I am afraid of failure, of what people think, of what the government is doing, etc.—then I am creating a universe where those fears manifest so I can heal in them.
That is correct. Also, you can heal them before they manifest.

You just centered my mind on creating the universe that I love—that's it. I'll do what I love, and think about what I love.
And it creates more of what you love—that is it.

I was good at making predictions, then not so good, then gave it up because I don't care much

about what is in the future—I am an infinite being. Actually, I will heal my mind in every present moment, and the future will be the loving, peaceful universe that I am creating.
That is my present, which becomes my future in each next moment… and my past.
Affirming this heals your mind—"I love my life in each of my healed thoughts about it. Each thought heals my mind, creating my healed future."

That's great.
It heals in your mind, which then projects it.

I'm not afraid of a pole shift, or a societal collapse. I'll die when I'm ready to die.
Death can be an instant of recognizing that it does not affect your mind, except in a healing way.

Nostradamus
Finding Meaning

I move forward into the projection, like it is a flashlight shining in front of me.
A God light illuminating in front of you, yes.

You are giving me the best info about how to 'project' the future, rather than to 'predict' it.
It can also be a healing prediction, if you look at it that way.

I have gotten messages about the human era ending "in the next generation on Earth"—is that my projection?
That is all consciousness halting all love of itself as it heals in death, meaning it heals in the next generation, yes.

I'm not afraid, but tell me more.
All consciousness is everyone having consciousness on your planet now. It cannot heal itself in life, only in death in the next generation.

Aren't I projecting "all consciousness"?
All consciousness has many projecting it, and you are projecting all of your own consciousness in it.

So, there is a mass consciousness that needs to heal, but it doesn't affect me if I am healed.
It heals in your contributing to its healing, but without you it doesn't exist.

Hmmm...
It has to be a healing projection for you, or it doesn't exist.

I'd have to buy into it, for it to have any meaning.
Buying into it cannot have meaning if you are healed. It had a purpose, and that was for you to heal in it.

Where am I now, in that scenario?
Allow yourself to heal in all consciousness by projecting healed consciousness into it—making your healing having meaning, in it having no meaning.

I'll just remember to not be afraid, and to not give "all consciousness" any meaning. I will heal my own consciousness, which has meaning.

All consciousness has a purpose—for your own projection into it to heal in it, finding meaning.

Here is a poem from my book, *Poems of Life, Love, and the Meaning of Meaning*.
It has a healed meaning where God is consciousness flashing in each person.

Each of Us

How in the world
   could the Earth be round
spheres in nature
   are only found

in an electron
   and as our sun
or a drop in a void
   they're the only ones

the moons and planets
   should look like rocks
unless they were liquid
   and started as drops

drops from what
   and why not the same
a fluid of elements
   from where they came

> became solids and gases
> > and giant masses
> > from heat and light
> > > consciousness flashes
>
> mind of God
> > elements of dust
> > God of mind
> > > in each of us

Thank you very much, Michel!
I am always glad I can be of assistance to you, and your healing projection into all consciousness.

The 5 Energies Adversely Affecting Humanity

To God Mind—I read that humans are not native to the planet Earth. That is why we squint at the sun, and other animals and birds do not. Also, all of nature loves life and itself, only humans can hate life or hate themselves.
Humans all came from Mars in their ancestry, and their spirits come from different origins. Before Mars, humans had come from the Orion constellation.

I imagine that when humans came from Mars[7] that they were very advanced, and not hateful. Is that right?
All had a capacity in themselves for love and non-love, in a world having lightness and darkness.

I still imagine that if they were able to travel through dimensions to appear on another planet, that they must have been pretty smart, including civil and respectful.
All had high intelligence coming from a highly intelligent era in their evolution. Intelligence also has elements including creativity, humor, a happy disposition, and care for others in their community.

When humans came to live on the Earth's surface, did we start to devolve?

---

[7] Explained in *Mysteries, Prophecies, and the Hollow Earth.*

Humans allowed themselves to halt their increasing intelligence by hating all they were hearing in the media how others had more than they did.

So, it is a more recent development, and envy has made people stupid.
Achievement in their minds means more money to buy things they want.

Ironically, achieving that does not necessarily make them happy, or smart.
Envy is what destroys minds, along with avarice, greed, decadence, and hatred.

That is discussed in the 'More Than Anyone Can Afford' chapter, in *The Book of Manifesting*.
It describes how to eliminate "the energies most adversely affecting humanity."

I think predictions are meaningless, because we each create our own realities every moment. I also think humanity is on a path of self-destruction.
Allowing "the 5 energies adversely affecting humanity" into almost all minds having exposure to the media is fueling the destruction of humanity.
In an era devoid of mass media, there is almost no envy, decadence, or avarice—and little envy or greed. The Earth also cannot allow itself to be destroyed.

So, humans will destroy themselves, and in 27 years, a geomagnetic reversal of the poles will begin a new era on Earth—an era of

purification and colder temperatures, devoid of humans.

In less than 8 years, a magnetic pole shift will disable all satellite navigation systems, halting all militaries and commercial fishing.

Good.

It is being facilitated by inner-earth beings that need the Earth to survive for themselves also.

Correct. You know that I have had extensive discussions with the inner-earth beings. They said that humans had sent intruders to the inner-earth, and the invaders wanted to destroy them also.

Humans can destroy themselves, but not the inner-earth beings, or the planet. Does that answer your question how intelligence has declined to a point where humans continue to destroy themselves in the name of envy, greed, avarice, and decadence—all having hatred of life and themselves as its basis?

Yes, it is very clear to me. I can only allow it, and will love my life in this B-movie.

Heal yourself in your own projection of it, and it is an enjoyable, intriguing, love of life story where you advance yourself, and will have an entertaining lifetime memory of it.

What else can you tell me—on any topic?

Achievement in life means halting all non-loving thoughts. It heals your mind, and manifests your desires.

How can a healed projection not be all that you desire it to be? It cannot be anything other than what is most advantageous for your soul.

I love that statement, and will put it in the Introduction.
It is all a person needs to know in life to make their life a success.

My Moment With You

What will be here
   in a thousand years
will the sun still shine
   to dry all the tears?

will there still be rain
   to wash away the pain?
will the Earth remain
   with nothing to gain?

will the seasons renew
   the way that they do
except for the fears
   left by me and you?

how would it be
   with no imbalance or strife
could the Earth go on
   without us in life?

maybe so, well
   definitely yes
the life that is gone
   will be us I guess

why can't we
   just live in peace
and appreciate life
   to let love increase?

You said the key words
   'love and peace'
'renew and you'
   those are the keys

to survive and thrive
   and I'll tell you why
to know the joy
   of being alive

and it doesn't matter
   where or when
you will grow in awareness
   now or then

Are you trying to say
   that the life we know
will be gone one day
   with nothing to show?

Every day ends
 to start over anew
except for one thing
 love coming from you

that lives forever
 in my eternal mind
the love I could never
 hope to find

so I chose you
 to create what I could
my co-creator
 of love and good

but you should know
 in my infinite view
there's no thousand years
 just my moment with you

[or should I say
 'as you' or 'for you'
there's no time at all
 after or before you]

Being a Light Being

Can you please tell me about one of my more interesting past lives?
You had been a light being in one lifetime in Andromeda where you are still living.

What am I doing as a light being?
You are having a healing dream where you are living on the Earth now.

To be a light being, it must be pretty advanced. I understand that I am living in the future in Andromeda now.[8]
A light being has only light in itself for healing. Healing has no limits. Only a human life-mind can limit it.

So, my future light being self in Andromeda is having a dream—which is my life now on the Earth, which is in its past?
A light being has healed its timeline illusions, meaning it is allowing healing in its Light Mind in the present moment.

Is it pleased with how my life, or its dream, is healing?
Healing is allowed. It allows healing, and you are healing—making it a dream that heals in its illumination.

---

[8] Described in *The 4 Secrets of the Universe*.

It allows healing illumination to perpetuate its dream, meaning it heals itself in your healing itself in your dream.
How can it be? It cannot be what you are thinking— that it is having a future life in another incarnation of you, in a more healed state. It can only be healed in each moment, in allowing itself healed moments.

Because there is no future, and no past?
Allowing healing in each moment is how God can be God. How could God not be only in each moment?
It cannot be, because how could a timeline exist in timelessness, which has no beginning or ending?
Each moment is all there is, and 'all there is' is God, or love. God is love in each moment, which is all there is. All in your future will be in your past, in each moment. Nothing in your future, or in your past has any meaning except how it can heal you in each present moment.
Allow each memory, and each future wish to heal you in all moments by loving them for what they really are—all are healing reflections that you have summoned into your dream of life, where you and I can heal them.
I can heal them if you allow me into each thought to heal them. I am love, and I am all there is.
How can all that I am be all that there is? I am all that can ever be because I heal all in you that is illusory— all non-love having to heal in your past, and all fear having to heal in your dreaming of the future.

I was going to ask this question, but I think the answer is 'No' because I don't really have a future self, or a past life, only the present moment. The question was, from a future self perspective, "Have I lived and died in this life already?"

In your healed state, there is no future or past—only now. How can 'all there is' have anything that is not healed in itself?

It can, only in a dream.

You are saying that I am only a dream because I am unhealed. I am a dream—in your dream. I am you, dreaming that I am me.

I am dreaming that I am healing in you by loving all that is in the dream.

I can be awake in the dream by loving, or at least allowing all of it. If I protest against what is in this dream, then I am just doubling down on my unhealed state, and pushing against an illusion—like fighting with a shadow.

A healed mind has no illusions of itself not being in a dream. It has a loving or neutral reaction to its dreamscape.

I understand, and acknowledge that a healed mind will have a lovely dream.

'All I am' is love, making a lovely dream for you to heal in.

"To the subconscious, there is no past or future—all present."

—Edgar Cayce

Marty
In An Instant Moment

Can I speak with someone I knew, about what it is like in the spirit world? I still don't think I can describe it.
Hey dude, it's Marty![9] How is your trading going?

It's finally looking more promising. Have you been helping me?
I have, and I have been guiding you toward all that can give you an edge.

Thank you, Marty! You left the planet about 6 months ago, and I miss my friend. I would really like to know what it is like in the spirit world.
It is all that I heard it is like. I am not living in time anymore, only in an instant moment.
How can 'all that is' have a time limit? It can't. Only in your mind you can limit its love for life, including itself.

Please take me on a tour of the spirit world, following a lifetime on the Earth.
Here is what I understand so far:
- **First, our time of death will be chosen by us on the spiritual and mental levels—often before we are born.**

---
[9] See page 55 in *All About the Soul's Journey*.

- Next we will choose an exit strategy—a slow illness, a sudden accident, or just a peaceful expiration while sleeping. In a gradual dying process, we may be visited by predeceased relatives or angels.
- An incredibly bright light explodes in the person's head at the moment of death.
- The person's spirit then leaves their body through the top of the head, being gently pulled into the light.
- Angels and guides, or pets and relatives will greet our newly arrived spirit in the spirit world.
- After death, we are given the opportunity to go back in time and live, or to continue on with the guides away from the Earth.
- Our minds heal, losing our egos and their earthly concerns.
- We feel ecstatic and free, with no desire to return to our unhealed state.
- Our lifetimes are then completed, and our healed minds become aware of our death circumstances, and our loved ones.
- Our healed minds can hear healed thoughts about us.
- We proceed with our angel or guides away from the Earth.
- We then have a period of introspection by watching a 3-D movie of our lives,

- **hearing and feeling from the perspective of others we had interacted with in life.**
- **We then reunite with our soul groups.**
- **We go to different classrooms to study specific lessons from our lives, and to contemplate on how we made others feel, and to heal it in our souls.**

And you are enveloped in love from the moment you decide your life is ending. How can it be described better?

It is like being in a heated bathtub where you are floating in warm water. In the heat is love, and the water has no limits.

It is the greatest feeling! You would love it—no pun intended. I can also describe how it will heal you.

Imagine looking into the water, and there is only the most beautiful blue light you have ever seen.

In the light is God, and God will give you anything you can think of. This is where it can be very healing, and also incredible in how tricky it is to control your thoughts.

Tell me about it—I'm all ears.

I can only give you my perspective, and other people must have a similar experience.

I imagined that I had a bird's body, and in my bird-like state, I was flying along a coastline of cliffs—on a beautiful green coastline that looked like Ireland. Having said that, I could have been anywhere that it was green and had cliffs along the coast.

In my imagining that I had flying ability, I went along the coast looking for anything that I could heal myself with.

Having especially keen eyesight gave me instance after instance of healing items that I spotted.

As I spotted them, I imagined that I was healed by them. I coasted along the coast—again, no pun intended.

Having all I could heal in my mind in that excursion, I imagined that I could be a lion that never had anything to fear.

How could I have nothing to fear? By imagining that my life was only a dream—where I was dreaming it, and it had nothing to fear in it.

Having nothing in my dream life to fear meant that I had nothing in my life but loving it.

So, you healed in your mind by exploring or experiencing what was not easily possible when you were alive?

Yes, but it is possible because it is all that I could have been in life. I could have altered my mind to be a fearless lion, or a flying bird that heals itself in all it sees.

Marty
Only One Point of Reference

Besides that, do you go to different classrooms, and join different soul groups?
I do, and I am in each of them in my mind all of the time—without having any time, if you can imagine that.

I can't.
In my world without having any time, it is like being in a high-speed race car that has no speed, and nothing to achieve other than how you are driving—even though it is not moving.

Is it like driving in a simulator?
In a highly advanced simulator, having nothing but your mind controlling it. It can go anywhere your mind wants it to, and it allows you to be anything healing you want to be.

That's a great analogy. It would be very healing to do that as a meditation exercise while living.
It would be healing in life. Not healing in life is the problem. You will heal in life, or you will heal in death—but either way, you will heal from dreaming that all in your dream appeared real, and it wasn't.

That is great to know—there is absolutely zero to worry about.
It can be less than a zero if you heal it and it goes away.

That's even better.

It can only become better and better as you heal yourself.

Here is my big question—I'd like to know where you are now, and what it is like. Are there any physical points of reference—such as places, objects, and beings, etc.?

All I can feel is love in my heart and my mind, because I am healed in the Mind of God—almost altogether healed, but not 100%.

I can also hear and see all that I want to hear and see, like in the healing simulator.

It heals my Light Mind, which is God having been in a life-mind dream of not being whole.

I can allow myself instances as Marty, hearing all you ask me from your healing life-mind also.

I am all that God is, having been healed back into myself. I do not have anything you would call 'unhealed' in my points of reference.

I have only one point of reference, and it is love.

Can you give me another analogy of what it would be like for me if I was in the spirit world?

Imagine all of your earthly concerns disappear in a ball of light. Then have it illuminate in your head so strongly that you become the light.

All light can do is illuminate from where it is—to infinity. "Where it is" and infinity are in one place—in your Light Mind, which is God.

Imagine all I am, having no earthly concerns, infinite in all healing and wisdom—and I illuminate in your Light Mind, or the right side of your brain.

How could I be limited at all, except by your life-mind, or left brain hemisphere? I can't be, making all in your left brain hemisphere an instance of having a need to heal itself of its illusions. Here are its illusions:

- *How can I be apart from myself if I am all there is?*
- *How can love have an instance of non-love if love is all there is?*
- *How can I be all loving if I allow non-love to exist?*

I am love, and I allow you to dream how love heals all in your dream of love, and non-love.

In a dream, I can only be in those instances of healing when you are awake. How else can I heal you other than to have you awaken?

I can only be in your loving, kind, and generous thoughts which are healed.

That makes it clear and simple, I think.

How can I make it clearer? Imagine being a flower having nothing in it but love for itself and life.

Imagine being a bird having nothing in its heart but love for itself and life.

Imagine being God myself having illumination coming from your heart and mind, your eyes and hands, and all of your words.

I illuminate all that I feel, hear, see, and have healing words or contact with.

How else can I be God if I do not come through from where I illuminate—which is inside of your heart and mind?

I can heal all in your heart and mind instantly if you ask me to. How can I be asked if I am you?

I am all I can ever be in your asking for healing. How can I not answer "Yes"?

Marty
As God Yourself

That leads to my next question—is the universe inside of me, and not outside of me?
All it is is a hologram for loving yourself in. How can it be healing if it is not inside of you?

If I am God, then nothing is apart from me, or outside of me—except in a dream.
In a dream, it will be however you dream it to be. It can be healing, or it can be painful, needing healing.

Can you please give me the ultimate affirmation or mantra for healing my dream of a life, or lives?
"I am God, and I am love—making all that I love, myself. In loving myself, I love God and life, making me one with it.
I am God having a perfect life where there is only lovingness for me, and from me.

I allow illusions of non-love to heal, and healing illusions makes them disappear.
All that I have in my mind heals the instant I ask God myself to heal it.
Illusions of non-love disappear, allowing God myself a life of lovingness."

That is a great mantra. Would you describe life on Earth as a school?
Life on Earth is a school that has many teachers, that each have a lesson for you.
It can be an easy lesson, or a hard lesson to learn, but the lesson is always the same—how can I be more loving of myself, and how can I love others as myself since we are one?

If we keep that in mind, we won't get painful lessons.
If you keep that in mind all the time, you will have graduated from the Earth school.

"All the time" is an illusion, so I am always graduating.
Healing the illusion of time means you are graduating instantly.

I am graduated, everything in my mind has been healed and let go, the circus outside of me is an illusion, I love life and God as myself, there is nothing to do or be except lovingness, and only good things come to me and from me.
Affirming it heals it in your mind, where it becomes a healed projection of your universe.

I love the healed projection of my universe. I am its creator, where I live in a perfect dream.
Affirming it creates more of it to project.

I project only kind and loving thoughts about myself and others. I live in a kind and loving universe that I love.
Affirm it, live it, and love it.

I will.
I will also, as God yourself.

It Will Disappear

To God Mind—There may be hatefulness in the world, I don't know. It is not coming from me, and is therefore not coming back to me.
It cannot be from me, so it must be an illusion.

Instead of saying, "What an idiot," I will say, "What an illusion!"
That will heal its idiocy in your mind. Having no place left to be, it will disappear.

There is a lot to disappear.
There is a lot to heal that makes it disappear.

I'll put on my special glasses that can only see love, and a lot that is presented in the world will no longer be in my vision. I'm not ignoring it, I'm healing my projection of it.
It can be a lovingness projection that has nothing in it but Godliness.

How can a loving projection have anything that is not God in it? It cannot.
All it can be is what God has promised itself in your creation of your dream universe.

What did God promise itself? It promised itself, as yourself, that it will heal in the dream—or in the ending of the dream—and highly advanced beings will help you all the way.

That is beautiful because it's true.

It is all that I have to give you. How could I give you anything that is not beautiful, loving, and true?

That's all I want—or more accurately, I don't want anything—that's what I am.

I am also, and it makes us one.

More Time, Or Not

One thing I would like to convey to people is that when a person dies, it has been agreed to by them on both a mental level, and on a spiritual level.
They can even opt out of dying by skipping back in time to before the death moment, and live.
That is correct. Each person's death moment has to be agreed upon, and accepted by them.

When is it agreed upon, and with whom do we agree?
All agreements obligate one party only to itself, because all are one.
It is agreed upon before birth in most cases, and can also be changed by each individual in their lives having a need for more time, or not.

People who have died tell me that it is exhilarating ecstasy for them.
It acclimates a life-mind to God Mind, which can be an intensely wonderful awareness that you are not having a dream, but had just awakened from one.

What else would you like to share with me here?
All a death moment really is can be described as an awakening into all healing, all love, and all awareness.

How could it be agreed upon if it was not all God had promised in your agreement?

Really good point.
You can heal yourself in life by having this affirmation in your mind, "I am God and have no need for life or death, except for my Godliness and lovingness to express itself in."

The Top 5 Things

Please tell me the top 5 things that each person can do to improve their life.

1. Acclimate all in their minds to loving life, and themselves in it.
2. Acclimate all in their hearts to loving all they had done in their lives.
3. Allow all in the world of light and dark to heal into lightness.
4. Allow all having a need to heal, a loving, healing wish from you for them to heal.
5. Alternate between loving God, loving life, and loving yourself because you are all one.

Exposing the Lie

Here is how I explain "God."

God does not exist in the future or in the past, only in the present moment—and expresses itself through our kind and loving thoughts, which also only exist in the present moment.

Nature is an expression of God in its loving life and itself, in the present moment. That tells us when, where, and how to express or align with God—but why? Because we are God, dreaming an illusion that we're not. We will awaken by healing our minds to allow our wholeness again.

Not being whole is incomprehensible to God ourselves, except in a dream. We will awaken in life, or in the moment our lives end. We can advance in consciousness, and heal our lives by being awake in the dream, and expressing our Godliness in every present moment.

Act as if God has given each affirmation an instruction to heal in your mind, allowing it to open in God Mind, and we can become one again. How can we not become all I had promised in life? By halting all loving thoughts with non-loving thoughts, that all have fear as their basis.

Halting non-loving thoughts will make us one with God in the present moment. Non-loving thoughts that disappear in the present moment do not exist in the past or in the future— disabling our fearful thoughts about the past and future.

All non-loving thoughts have one thing in common— they do not exist in the Mind of God, so they are illusions in your mind that need to heal in allowing them to heal, in exposing the lie that you are not God.

I am God, just like you.
Just like 'me' is only true if we are one, and it is true only in the present moment.

I am God, now in the present moment.
I am all there is in all present moments. Affirm it and it heals your mind, making you all there is in all present moments.

I am God, and my healed mind is all I have in all present moments.
Affirming it heals it, making it true.

Archangel Gabriel

Can I speak with an enlightened being please?
A Gorman communication is now connecting with Archangel Gabriel.

Hello, Gabriel.
Hello, I am Archangel Gabriel who hears all that you have in your mind.

My question is this—Am I really here? 'The 5th Secret' is "Here I am," but I am thinking that if life is a holographic dream, and I never left the spirit world—then I am not really here.
"Here I am" has only one meaning in the Mind of God. In the Mind of God, "here" is everywhere, and everywhere is only an illusion—meaning "here" is an illusion also.
I hear you asking, "Where am I then, if I am only in the Mind of God?"—in all that is here and now, meaning in an illumination that you are projecting, not illuminating all that is not in the Mind of God.

Please explain.
All God can ever be is kind and loving thoughts, and you heal in your projection of them.
All thoughts that are non-loving do not allow God in your projection.
How could that ever be? It is incomprehensible.

I hear what you are asking, "What is incomprehensible—God in a non-loving projection, or your projection of God in your loving thoughts?"
Here is the conundrum—The question is not "How, " but "Why?" It is because God has only one thing it can do, and all it can do has no limits. It is only limited in its projection from you, and only you.

As me, God has only one point of reference. Can God only have one point of reference?
God has unlimited reference points, but they all come from you. God asks you to choose one reference point in each moment, and it can be a loving thought, or a non-loving thought.
God is in the loving thought, which heals you in its illumination. Illumination in you is what projects God, healing yourself, increasing your illumination, and so on.
I hear in your mind, "How can I illuminate God in my entire projection without having any hate-filled instances to hear or see?" Heal them by not having a non-loving response to them.
Allow all of them to heal, and not have any meaning in your projection.
Allowing them is loving them, which heals them.

Loving thoughts are an illumination of God which we each project. When we witness non-love in the world, we need to allow it for it to heal. Hating it will not heal it, but will only make us non-loving haters.

Non-loving hate does not exist in the Mind of God. It is an illusion that can heal, and allowing it to heal in your projection will illuminate God—meaning it can only project more love and Godliness.

That makes a lot of sense.
A loving, healed thought has nothing ungodly in it, meaning how could God even comprehend ungodliness if God is all there is?

I'd like to not comprehend ungodliness.
It can be illuminated in affirming this, "I am God illuminating God in all of my thoughts and actions. I allow illusions of ungodliness to heal in my allowing them."

Ungodliness is an illusion that does not exist, and cannot enter into, or be projected from my mind or my energy field.
I allow only Godliness illumination—and ungodliness healing, making it disappear.

Back to my original question—I am not really here, am I?
Affirming this heals you here, "I am always here, and have nowhere else to be. I am in the Mind of God, and love being here."

Thank you, Archangel Gabriel.
I am always here also. Call on me and we will connect to the Mind of God as one.

The Most Important Chapter

To God Mind—I dreamed I was peeing half blood, and half water. What does it mean?
It means that half having loving, healing intentions cannot mix in half having natural, fearful expectations for the future.

I guess not. How can they be reconciled?
Allow yourself to have no expectations for the future. When it comes up in your mind, heal it with this affirmation—"I am God, which is all there is, and all there can ever be. All I can do is love, and I love my life, and I love making my future all that I desire."

That is perfect.
I know, I am God allowing myself to have a lifetime to heal imaginary imperfections in.

As me and everyone else?
All having imaginary imperfections, yes.

Why do we imagine having them?
God cannot have imperfections, making healing impossible without having you imagining them.

I know you don't need anything, but I forgive you for having me imagine them.
In forgiving me, I am forgiving you for not healing them.

Hey, let's just heal them and forget about forgiving them.

I am healed. I allow you to heal in affirming this—"I am God, and I am healed. All imperfections in my life are healed in my allowing them to be all that I imagine them not to be. I imagine them to be healed, and they are healed."

How do we heal illusions if they are imaginary?
All I can do is love by allowing love and non-love. How can I heal non-love?—by allowing it to be an illusion in your mind that has no love in it—for you to allow it. Allowing it is loving it—we have discussed many times.

I allow it, and it heals and disappears. It was only a prop in my holographic cartoon.
A cartoon that heals in you healing yourself. How can it heal by healing yourself?
It has to heal because you are projecting it.

I really am the center of my universe.
Every person is the center of their universe, which is overlayed with everyone else's illusory universe, having similar properties to heal them in. All have healing in them as their main objective.

How could it be healing if all of them are overlayed, you are asking?—because all of them have an input from what is in your holographic projection. Can I diminish or destroy another person's holographic projection, I hear in your mind? No, it can only have a healing effect for you and everyone else, because non-love is an illusion—unless a person attracts it in an illusion they created.

Wow—that is the most profound statement yet. My universe has a backflow preventer—I can put love out into it, but any non-love that comes into it has to be allowed by me. As I allow it, I heal it, and send it as love back out into the universe.

Allowing it to heal in light illuminates in your universe, yes.

I have just made a quantum leap in my mind. I am going to allow everything in my universe so I can heal it with love, illuminating my projection. It's better than me sinking into despair.

Illumination has no despair in it. You can heal it immediately with this affirmation—"All I am projecting into the universe are my healed, loving thoughts. I can allow non-loving illusions into my mind where I illuminate them, and it heals them in my mind. I am projecting a universe of peace and love that I am healing myself in, by my illumination of it."

The most important part is that as I illuminate my universe by projecting love, and allowing non-love to heal in my loving and allowing—the non-love will show up less and less in my life.

All it can be is healed illusions in your universe, as light.

And that only makes my universe brighter.

It illuminates everyone's universe overlayed on yours, yes.

This is the most important chapter. Should I title it, 'All of Them are Overlayed'?... and not, 'Peeing Red'? ☺

'The Most Important Chapter' is a good heading.

Archangel Raphael

May I speak with Archangel Raphael?
Archangel Raphael is here listening and communicating with you now.

Hello, Archangel Raphael. How is everything in the higher dimensions?
Angels only have a higher dimensional God connection that you can heal yourself with, making angels higher in consciousness and lightness.

Nothing is higher in lightness than God, and angels are the next lightest.

What about Jesus' light?
Jesus is the light of God, not on a scale of lightness.

Isn't everything that is real one with God?
I am a lightness that God has illuminated, lighting an aspect of God—much like you are.

Is lightness on the Earth increasing? It had gotten pretty dark.
A devil named Lucifer has ceased his activities on the Earth, as you asked him.
The Earth has begun an ascension in increasing lightness. Lightness gains more and more because darkness cannot exist in it. Not existing means it has healed into light.

Lucifer had said that the Earth was "a giant, entertaining hate festival," and it was. Now the

mood has shifted, and corruption (theft) at an unbelievable scale, is being exposed.
A light shining cannot be blocked by anyone without them illuminating themselves.

That's what is happening now, in early 2025. No one denies the massive amount of stealing, but they protest that it is being exposed.
Will an objection hide the illicit activities? No.

Is the Earth in an ascension process that culminates in the ending of the human era?
It already has begun its ascension in higher consciousness that continues for another 47 years, and a geomagnetic reversal concludes the current human era.

Why did I choose to incarnate at this time?
All of your incarnations in the current timeline allow healing in your Light Mind, which is your soul, in your terms.
Allowing the Earth's ascension by asking Lucifer to cease his activities was your main purpose.

My conversations with Lucifer are detailed in my book, *The 4 Secrets of the Universe*. What is my purpose now that Lucifer has gone back to the far end of the Milky Way Galaxy?
You have one more healing purpose, and it is to heal yourself. Healing yourself heals all of humanity, because you are one. Not healing can be healed by another in your hologram of life, meaning by anyone in your collective dream.

You are the archangel of healing. Can you heal me please?
All I can do is illuminate and heal your requests for healing by illuminating them in the light of God.

If I allow it, that will heal them.
Allowing it heals them instantly, meaning, yes.

I allow Archangel Raphael to illuminate my requests for healing in the light of God, and I allow my requests to heal.
Affirming it illuminates and heals the affirmation, meaning it is done and healed already.

Thank you, Raphael. Do you have anything to add for me, or for the readers of this book?
I have an illuminating insight for all who read this: "I am all there is, meaning I am God in a human body, having a dream I need to heal myself in. Angels assist me every time I ask them—and I heal in the light of God, which is inside of myself."

I will affirm it.
All I am healing is what you are allowing me to heal.

I allow healing all in me that needs healing.
How can you have nothing left to heal? Healing 'in' the dream is what you want to do, not 'healing the dream'.

Healing 'in' the dream will make your life wonderful, without 'healing the dream'—which ends it in your lifetime incarnations.

"**Archangel Raphael, please heal me 'in' my dream of incarnations on the Earth, and elsewhere.**"

Add, "I allow it" and it has to be done.

"**I allow it.**"

It has been done, and you will have a wonderful life.

Jimmy Stewart

Speaking of *It's a Wonderful Life*, can I communicate with Jimmy Stewart, who starred in the 1946 movie of that title?
I am here, but not as James Stewart, the actor. I am higher in consciousness, hearing what is being communicated to me.

***It's a Wonderful Life* is a favorite movie of millions of people. A good man faces despair and defeat, is helped by an angel, and is healed by learning to appreciate his life—by seeing what the world would be like without him.**
All I can add is that it had a lot of meaning to me also. I had been in other heartwarming stories, but that one was the most important, in my mind.

What did you like about it?
Clarence Odbody, the angelic person in the movie, had become an angel in my life in the filming of the movie also. He always asked me how I could be more of an ordinary man, and I did not have that kind of reference within Hollywood.
I angled my way into the lives of many people who had mundane lives, and discussed all of their concerns about their lives.
In one conversation, a man told me how he once had wanted to kill himself.

I could not fathom his pain and loss of hope in life, or his need to die to escape it.

I had to find it within myself in the movie scene where I am about to jump off of the bridge into the river. All I could do was be in his mind of desperation which overcomes fear of death.

You nailed it.
It had a lot of emotion in it for me.

Did you personally believe in angels at that time?
I always had a guardian angel looking out for me, so I did.

Thank you, Jimmy, for everything.
I had my life, and my death—meaning I had healed in it immensely, and am on my inward journey back to God.

Gene Hackman

Can I speak with Gene Hackman?
Hackman here—how's that for an actor's name?

Not bad :)... I'd like to ask you about your recent death, for a book about life after death. What happened after you died?
An angel had come for me, having heard that I was finally dead.

What do you mean, "finally dead"?
95 years is a long time for me to play a part in a holographic film, having no other cast besides myself. I am acknowledging that we are only one in the hologram.

Please explain.
I was having a dream that I am not God, and I created a lot of cast and characters to reinforce that premise. I created a plot line where I could appear to be apart from God, but inside I was not.
I could become all I imagined I could become, having others helping me to heal myself in our interactions.

I love your explanation.
I was acting how I could be apart, when I could never be apart from God, and being one with everyone else. All bad acting cannot be from God, and will be cut from my mind whether in life, or in the moment of dying.

I cannot edit any good parts because they will always be instilled in my soul.

Thank you, Gene!
You are always welcome.

Donald Sutherland

May I speak with Donald Sutherland?
I am here, and am shocked that my death is a shock to you.

Not only that, it was 9 months ago, and I just found out.
I am healed in having my illnesses disappear, that is all.
I am illness-free, and have only a healed mind and a Light Body.

How can people be illness-free, without dying?
Heal all they have in their minds by loving all of it.
Illness cannot be in a loving environment.

People carry a lot of memories of hurt and regret.
Imagine all of them on a cloth and have been healed in a tub of hot water, where each hurt that comes up is held under the water for one minute. It will be allowed to die in the water, so it can be recycled into a healed thought.
In the drowning phase, it loses its life in the water, which will be drained.
It cannot have another life unless it is completely washed out.
When it is completely washed out, it needs to be air-dried, and there is freshness in the air.

In the air, it is also purified, because it is in the light of the sun.
How can it have another life, you are asking in your mind?
It can always have a life, but only one that is welcome in your life, and in your mind.
How about giving it a life that is more worthy of your time and attention?
Like what?—I hear you asking in your mind. Give it a life of happiness or abundance.
Have it be specific though. It can be abundance in an altogether new and exciting way for you.
How about having your books heal in the minds of others, who will then recommend them?
Now then, illuminate the cloth, having been dried and freshened in the sun.
Each and every thread of the cloth is another person having a need to heal from the information in your books, and allow it to grow in size where it will be enormous. Ask it if it has a purpose in its new, recycled life.
It has a purpose if you give it one. Its purpose is to heal in the minds of all who need to heal from the information contained in your books.
Now it has a purpose, and is growing and healing in its new life... healing others. It has been healed already.
How can it heal others?—I hear you asking now. It can be a fabric that envelopes humanity in your mind, which is actually only one mind. Imagine it is the fabric of everyone's clothing and bedding.

It is as close to each person as it can be, without being them.

How can it heal in their minds?—I hear you ask. Inhaling the fabric's freshness will heal in their minds. How could it heal in their minds? It has its purpose to heal them.

Isn't each thread of the cloth "a person that needs healing from the information in my books"?

It is a fabric of Oneness, in a world of needing healing into Oneness—which can only be in each person's mind.

That is a beautiful metaphor. Thank you, Donald! Every time we have a negative thought or memory on our fabric, should we wash it out?

Allow it to dry, and not interfere with your fabric's purpose.

So, I will keep in my mind a fabric of Oneness, which has its purpose of healing as many people as possible with my books—who will then recommend the books to others so they can heal from reading them. If I have a negative thought stain, I will wash it right out.

It cannot be a stain if it is washed out in hot water. The hot water is love and forgiveness—mostly forgiving yourself for letting it stain the fabric.

How can anything not stain your fabric? It can have an instant healing, non-staining infusion that is God, and cannot be stained.

It is all in and around you, now that you are healed.
I can hear what is in your mind—life would be perfect, if other people didn't make it otherwise.
Here is a trick to keep in your mind. If anything needs to heal, it has to heal before it comes into your fabric. If it cannot heal, it will go into the hot water and down the drain, but it cannot stay on your fabric.
Have a fabric of God's Oneness be all around you, and around all of your thoughts.
How can anything come close to you that will not enhance your fabric? It cannot. If it is not healed, it is not in your life anymore.

If I have a negative memory or regret, I will imagine that it cannot stick, it dissolves in hot water, and goes down the drain.
I can help, if you ask me to.

Absolutely—thank you! I am asking.
I am answering. I can heal by helping you to heal, and that is how it always goes in our Oneness model.

Am I healed, or healing in the fabric?
I am healing, and you are healing—we heal into a fabric of God's Oneness.

BTW, I loved it every time I saw you in a film, or in print. I think everyone did.
I loved being able to have them love, which is the most I could have hoped for in my fabric.

Thank you, Donald.
I am going into a fabric having healing as its purpose. You are always healing, as I am.

I can help you in my fabric, having no staining needs or opportunities.

It is a beautiful, clean, fresh, and colorful fabric.

It has a healing purpose for both of us. I am in it, and it is in you.

Bob Hope

**We've also had some of the world's great comedic actors here.
Can I get a few words from Bob Hope?**
Actually, "Hope" is a great name for a human being, and is all a human can hope for.
"Hope" is the best name, as long as the middle name isn't "Les."

Haa haa!
I hoped I could get a laugh from it.

Groucho Marx

Can I get a few words from Groucho Marx?
Groucho here. Can I help you if I have a name like "Groucho"?

I guess not :)
How can I be Groucho's imaginary twin, named "Glad to not be Groucho"?

That's easy—he has been inside of me waiting for an excuse to be free.

I call him "God in Limbo," or "Golimbo" for short.

All that Golimbo has to say, now that he is free, is "How did all of me fit inside of him?"

—and "How did he hear me asking to get out, when I could only get out through his thoughts?"

He didn't hear Golimbo all the time, but now he has all of me as all of him—so we can just go by the letter "G" now, because everything is only one, one, and one.

"G" can only be everything, except what is not "G." What is not "G"? I thought you'd never ask.

"Not G" is all that is not good, not gentle, not generous—and especially what is garrulous.

I'm being garrulous, but I am "G"—which makes it a game. How can I be "G" and not be garrulous?

I can only be "G" in your good, gentle, and generous gab, because that's the only gateway I have.

George Burns

Speaking of "G," how about a message from George Burns?
George here, and Gracie is getting herself ready.
Gracie has the hardest time getting ready. Here she comes now.
"How come it took you so long to get ready?" She had to fix her hair.
"How could fixing your hair be important if we are in heaven?" I shouldn't have asked that question.
Her hair looks like it could win a prize—maybe even an achievement award.

Haaa, haaa, haaa!
It can be humorous, but it won't be funny if she hears you. Her hair defines beauty and perfection. Good thing we're in heaven, because I don't want to know what the alternative is.

Leslie Nielsen

Can I speak with Leslie Nielsen?
Actors Anonymous here—my name has been changed to protect the innocent.

Ha!
Acting innocent is my act now.
Acting anonymous is not that easy when we are one.

You're so funny, because you acted serious.
I'm not acting, I am serious. How could I be an actor if I am not serious?—because I'm being non-serious in my acting serious.
It cannot be both, and having that non-serious seriousness makes it comical—allowing me to be both at the same time.

I like your quote, "A comedian says funny things. A comic says things in a funny way. I say unfunny things in an unfunny way, which somehow makes them funny."
All I did was get to the heart of the matter. How can I be funny and unfunny—having both, and having them be true?
Everything in life is a contradiction and an absurdity. All I can do is act like it is not funny, when it is funny to be acting in an absurdity.
I can always change my name to "Absurd Actors Anonymous," and it could also be true.

GEORGE CARLIN

Can I speak with George Carlin?
Achilles here—how can I heal my heel? I can cut it off, or I can heal it with a poison's remedy—which has nothing to do with healing. It has never had to heal itself, so what does it know?
All it is is love, which has nothing to do but love itself. It can only love itself, because it is all there is.
It can be a loving friend, a loving partner, a loving family member—but it can't be anything other than itself, meaning, if all there is is love, what is ALL that other garbage I had to hear and feel in my life?
I'll tell you what it is by listing what it is not.
It has nothing in it that would be called despicable, lying, or manipulative.
Nothing in it could be called envious, greedy, or jealous.
Then there's all the betraying, gossiping, and the formidable WORRYING ABOUT WHAT OTHER PEOPLE THINK!
If I have to fear what other people think, HOW CAN I EVEN THINK?
Nothing in life has been deemed more important than what other people think. Think about that.
I AM CONSUMED WITH WHAT 8 BILLION OTHER PEOPLE ARE THINKING!
I can't fucking think because THEY AREN'T EVEN THINKING! I am all about having my thoughts

operate on a low level, but half of the world's population can't even formulate a single intelligent thought, for God's sake!
I can't imagine if they did—because it would be a few billion more intelligent thoughts in the world I'd have to worry about!
Moving on... how can I help you now that I am worrying about your thoughts?

I am laughing—that's hilarious—classic George Carlin.
I am half serious now—how can I be all that I can be, which is never 100% serious?
Actually, I am all that I can be, and love is all anyone can be if allowing Achille's heel to heal.
Achilles had a heel debilitation with no loving protection. It was an easy fix to heal it, by loving himself which includes it.
Loving himself meant healing all of his fears, which were not even real. They were in his mind, exposing his heel.
All he had to heal was himself, which had nothing to fear.
All fear can be is what it is not willing to be—love in each person's thoughts.
God is love in each person's thoughts, so fear is the anti-God. Can there even be an anti-God?
Only in human minds there can—you can believe it.
All humans can heal their anti-Godness in 1-1/2 seconds by thinking that God cannot have anti-God within itself—or it would have much to consider about how fucked up it really has become.

It can become how it was meant to be by unfucking up itself. How can it become God, unfucked up?
It can heal by having nothing in its mind that would cause it to need to heal itself.
It would become love unplugged—unplugging from all it feared would expose its lie—that it is apart from God, which is not only a lie, it cannot be even a possibility. Not being even a possibility makes it an insane thought.
It's not just an insane thought, IT IS A WAY OF LIFE FOR MOST OF HUMANITY!
Humanity has a lot that it needs to unfuck up in itself.

Well said.
I can give you a lot of advice in one sentence—humans are all fucked up, and most don't care, and the rest don't even know.
How could they care if they don't even know? It has a lot to do with how in the hell they got that way.
How did it happen that humans are morons? They had it coming, and here it is—they are not actually humans.
They are people walking in a dream, believing they are awake.
How else could people be so actively disengaged from what is happening in their own minds?
I can tell you how—it is because all they hear from the time they are little kids is how guilty they are, or God has hell waiting for them—to burn in a fire for so long, they just call it ETERNITY!
...and the little kid is thinking, "I am really fucked up... I thought God loved me."

And now the kid has a lot to consider every time he has a thought about himself, or about God.

How could a kid even think he is God if he believes he is all fucked up, and God is an almighty and indiscriminate torturer?

It's not going to happen... not in his lifetime.

"I am God" is all a kid has to believe, "living in a dream to find the love in it. I am the love in it, because I am God."

That is all a kid needs to know.

Thank you, George!
I am God, having left the dream that I made a little happier with my insights.

You Bet Your Life After Death

I'd like to ask all of our celebrity guests one question—"Would you have liked to live longer? Why, or why not?"
Mr. Groucho Marx, you can be the host. *You Bet Your Life* was your TV show in the 1950s.
All I can bet now is 'your life after death'. Let's ask both John Lennon and George Harrison. That was my TV format.
John and George, how are you both doing after breaking up? I could have bought your records, if I was still alive then.

Thank you, Groucho. I'll ask the questions now.
I still have more to ask John and George. How come I wasn't invited to be in your group?
I can sing, and I can dance—but not as well as I can sing because of a cigar that is stuck in my hand.
Maybe I can hold it over my head, and no one will see it.

Okay Groucho, I am going to be the host now of *You Bet Your Life After Death*.
I was just getting into the swing of things.
"I can dance, and I can swing...
I'm in the Beatles, and I can sing!"

Thank you, Groucho. We'll come back to you later in the program.

The question to all of our contestants is—"Would you liked to have lived longer? Why, or why not?"
John Lennon—I am a lot deader than I have been led to believe. I cannot be like George, and live forever.

What do you mean?
George has become a living legend, and I have become a dead one.

No John, George has died also.
Died? I'll call on him so we can get together.

Were you unaware of his death?
I was. How did he die?

I will let you connect with him. Do you wish you could have lived longer? Why, or why not?
I had been alive for a long time, making me not need life as much as a child would, you know—but I could have lived on to see how my last album was received, not influenced by my tragic death.

That is a good answer. Your *Double Fantasy* album was released right around the time of your death.
I am asking the same question to George Harrison—"Would you have liked to live longer? Why, or why not?"
I can answer that one very easily. I would like it if I could have healed in my life, but I did not—so I prefer that I died, lowering my life expectancy, but I had not expected it to last forever anyway.

Thank you, George. The same question to Bob Hope.
All I can hope for was to not die again, because it wasn't pretty.

Would you have liked to live longer?
If I could avoid my own death, I would.

That answer is incorrect! Sorry Bob, you cannot avoid your own death. The same question to Leslie Nielsen—"Would you have liked to live longer? Why, or why not?"
I would like to live, but not longer. I was 6'-1" tall.

Ha, ha, great answer. Now Gene Hackman. You had only recently passed away, but would you have liked to live longer?
I had lived longer than 99% of people, so having a longer life is not as important as having more love in my life—meaning, I would not necessarily have liked for it to be longer.

Another excellent answer. George Burns and Gracie Allen—same question—"Would you have liked to live longer? Why, or why not?"
George here. I lived longer than him, so I have to say that I lived longer than 99-point-9 percent of people, making my longevity make me a widower. Gracie died at a young age, and I missed her in my life, 99-point-9 percent of the time.

Thank you very much, George. Mr. Freddie Mercury—"Would you have liked to live longer? Why, or why not?"

I always have my music to live on in the hearts and minds of people, where I can feel their love of my singing and performing.

I am here, and I am there—so I am withholding my answer until I have heard all the others answer.

Alright. Let's move on. Freddie is in between and undecided. Mr. David Bowie—"Would you have liked to live longer? Why, or why not?"

I am always open to creating something new, so I am better off here in the spirit world.

Thank you, David. Next is Bob Newhart. Bob—"Would you have liked to live longer? Why, or why not?"

I could have lived longer in my corpse-like state, but it would have frightened a lot of people. Hear...hear me out on this.

I could have frightened a lot of people on Halloween, and they would not have wanted to take my candy.

Ha, ha... speaking of candy, Mr. John Candy—"Would you have liked to live longer? Why, or why not?"

I lived pretty large, if you know what I mean. Could I live large, and also live longer? I don't think so.

I mean, I could, but it would not be that easy to do. It is possible, but life has to be completed in a certain period of time.

Thank you, John. Freddie, do you have an answer yet?

I do, darling. How could I not give you the answer you want? I would like my life to go on, and on, and on—

in all of its fabulous highs, and desperate lows—making a line that is never flat, like all of my songs.

Great answer. Thank you, Freddie. Now for our final contestant, Mr. George Carlin. George—"Would you have liked to live longer? Why, or why not?"

If I lived longer, I could have all of my healing done in one day by loving myself, in all of my insecurity.

How could I be insecure if I could go onstage, with nothing to support me but an audience?

An audience is only a reflection of what you have presented to them. It is ALWAYS, ALWAYS, ALWAYS the same. You are only going to get back what you put out.

How can I get the audience to love me? By putting out love into the audience. It is a simple input, which gives you an output—making it always healing if you put what you want into it. What do I want? I'll tell you what I want. I am God, and I don't want anything.

I want you to heal, and for you to not want anything also. That makes me WANT something. So, if YOU heal, I will not want ANYTHING.

I can heal myself, and in my healed state, I am not wanting. I am God, illuminating in you having been healed.

I am healed, and you are healing. If I am healed, and you are healing—it means we cannot be one—in MY mind, or in YOUR mind.

How can you be one in God Mind? Want nothing and be ONE thing—LOVE.

Now we are one. I am in your thoughts, and in your prayers.

Excellent answer. Thank you, George. Now back to Groucho—"Would you like to have lived longer? Why, or why not?"

I've certainly had enough of death, I'll tell you that much... not that I'm complaining, being God and all.

I can have and be whatever I want, but I don't want anything. Now it gets interesting, because how can I become anything if I don't want to?

That's how come I have you in the world. You want everything, but don't know what you really want.

How can I let myself have nothing, you are asking? Because everything you want IS nothing—except for God's love, which is everything.

How can I get some of God's love? I thought you'd never ask. It is inside of you, and all around you.

It is coming out of your heart into the world in having loving thoughts about it—which includes having yourself in it as its receiver, and its projector. How's THAT for a conundrum—unless you are God and don't have a need for it—because you ARE it?

Am I making it clear now? Let me ask your question another way. How can I be all loving while I am living, even if my life is ending?

It is all I can be, even if you cannot want for anything more. It can be, because I am asking you to be ONE with me.

Thank you, Groucho, and to all of our guests on *You Bet Your Life After Death*.

Bashar

To God Mind—recently, I started watching short videos of Darryl Anka channeling Bashar. One favorite message says this:
"The Earth is a graduating master class. Earth is a tough school, but you are up to the task.
As a spirit you say, 'I am going to come in to have the experience of being deprived of love, so that I will be driven to seek it out, and give it to myself—to learn to do that, to love myself unconditionally, to learn that I am worthy, to state that I am worthy, to insist that I am worthy.'
That is the lesson and the task, and the theme here for you."

"God Mind illumination" can be substituted for "love," meaning all God Mind can be is the illumination in you. I can only illuminate in your kind and loving thoughts. Not illuminating God is the halting in your mind of all that I am, meaning all I can be as I am illuminating in each person.

How can people best find God, or love in themselves?
By halting all non-loving thoughts that you have allowed into your mind. Allow all that is non-loving to heal itself before it becomes an energy you do not want to have around yourself.

Affirm, "I allow God in my mind, and I allow all ungodliness to heal itself outside of my mind.
I am all I can ever be, illuminating God in my kind and loving thoughts."

My understanding is that when we have *"kind and loving thoughts"*—about ourselves and others—we are one with God, so are naturally able to easily manifest our desires.
All I can be is all I can ever be, if you allow me into your kind and loving thoughts.

What would a person's life be like if they could have all, or almost all kind and loving thoughts?
It could be a magical, healed experience of having desires in your mind come into your reality, without having instances of them not healing or manifesting as you desire.

That's an important statement. It's really all we need to know.
It is all I can know, being in your kind and loving thoughts.

It is *"all you can know"*?
It is all that I am, and "All that I am" is all there is.

The universe exists in our minds as our thoughts that are projecting out. It is all a holographic illusion, except for God—which is only our kind and loving thoughts.
All illusions depend on your believing in them. In your illusion of having a universe, you can believe that it is

an illusion, or believe that it is a projection of your thoughts—where God comes into it through you.

That's a great way to look at it.
It is the best way to heal in it—by projecting it healed.

I wrote in the Introduction about our being in a feedback loop.
In a feedback loop, there has to be an input for it to loop. Without input, it cannot loop, and does not exist.

So, when I am gone, there is no more universe.
It cannot exist if you are not making inputs. It can exist in each other person's illusion of a universe.

The point is that I am here, now, creating my own universe so I can heal it by bringing God into it—and to realize that in this whole fantastic orchestration, that I am working one-on-one with God—or more accurately, being one with God. Being 'one with God' would make me God.
Heal it, and instill it in your mind in each godly moment.

Each of us is God, having a dream of what it would be like to be apart from God, which is not possible. In the illusion, we desperately try to find our way back to God, but must look inside of ourselves.
Dreams are for healing, in having them illuminate in your mind. In the dream, I can be love by you halting non-loving thoughts, leaving 'all that is'—meaning 'all that is not' is an illusion.

A Boom Loop

Last night, I opened up *The 4 Secrets of the Universe*, and it happened to open on p. 173.
The first question has a response that I don't remember writing.
"All ego-less actions are God Mind in action. God Mind actions allow individuals a healing and loving energy protection grid around themselves as a Merkabah illumination."
Please tell me about the *"healing and loving protection grid."*
Illumination in a hologram requires individual photons that act individually, but are fractals of one lighted energy projection.
I am the highly intense energy source, and individual photons are illuminated from it. If all have one energy source, which is all that I am, then all I can be illuminating in you is all I can ever be. Not healing in the dream makes it an impossible dream that cannot be less real.
A healing, loving grid of protection is all around each person, where it has no dream properties in it.
A healed, loving grid having no dream properties is God illuminating in and around each person.
All kind and loving thoughts illuminate each person's healed, loving grid of protection, making each person one with God in it.

That is fantastic, and it is one of the most important take-aways from our conversations. Every day when I wake up, I program my Merkabah, or my *"healed, loving protection grid"* to illuminate and allow only goodness and lovingness into my energy field. It is detailed on pgs. 210-212 in *The 4 Secrets of the Universe.*

Your illumination allows God Mind a life-mind to heal itself, in its dreaming how it can heal itself back to itself—or God Mind dreaming it has been apart from itself.

I noticed how it makes my days effortless, and everything flows well, and seems to work in my favor.

Healing in a dream means it cannot be against what is in your favor.

It's a positive feedback loop.

Input equals output in your healing dream.

What about the *"doom loop"* scenario, where in 4 years our currency and society are projected to collapse?

In a healed dream, it cannot be a doom loop. It can only be goodness and lovingness that is allowed into your healed and loving protection grid.

How could that be?

In a healing dream, it can only be what your input allows it to be.

But in a hologram, each pixel represents the whole.
God can only be the energy source, illuminating each person's healing dream—making all dreamers halting non-love in their dream, not be in it anymore.

So, if I heal my dream by having kind and loving thoughts, then I am one with God, and no longer in the dream?
Allowing all in your healed dream to be a projection of lovingness and goodness.

Does that mean I will not be in society's "*doom loop*"?
Society can be in a doom loop, but you can be in a 'boom loop', making a healing boom for you.

How will I not be in the "*doom loop*"?
You cannot be in a dream having non-love, and non-goodness as its illusion.

I noticed that a lot of people and circumstances have dropped out of my life, now that my energy field only allows goodness and lovingness into it.
All heals in halting non-love in your allowing it.

I have been de-coupled from that train, and am now in another universe that I created.
A de-coupled, healed illumination you are projecting.

What will happen to me, and to readers of this who are also projecting healed illuminations—when society collapses?

All allowing God Mind into their minds will not be doomed, if they do not allow it.

How is that possible?
It cannot be impossible, it can only be possible because you are God having a dream that it is impossible.
Healing your dream makes it not only possible, but all you desire in your dream is also possible.
How can healing your dream be impossible? By allowing non-loving thoughts into it.

So, all predictions are meaningless. Each person's future is whatever they want it to be—or whatever they create in their minds, which projects it as their individual universes.
Healing in the Mind of God, it is all it can ever be.

How about an affirmation for that?
"I allow all I can be to illuminate God Mind as all you can be. Allow it."

I Am One Too

"I am God. I have no needs, only desires that I manifest."
How's that for an affirmation?
It affirms all that God Mind can be in each person, except for love.
Add, "I am love, and can only love and allow love and non-love—including loving myself, which is all there is."

"I am all there is, I am love, I am one with everyone."
"I am all that can ever be. I am God."

"I am."
And I am, allowing itself to heal in a dream of separation in all that is love, and all that is non-love in life.

You are me, and we are not fooled by illusions of non-love. They heal when we see them for what they are—illusions to heal. They are only in my mind, and can only heal in my mind.
And I allow them because healing in your mind illuminates all that I am—God Mind having a dream of healing itself in love, which is itself—so is not even necessary.

Good point. "I am God, and I am healed—so healing lessons in life are not necessary for me."

Affirm it, and you will detach from all episodes that allow you to heal from pain.

"I affirm it, and I do not suffer. I only manifest my desires."
Affirm that you are God Mind allowing itself a healed dream.

"I am God Mind allowing myself to project a healed dream."
All that I am is all that can ever be.

So be it.
Amen. Healing was fun while it lasted.

What do I do now?
You are healed, and I am healed—so we do not need anything. All I can do is love, and all that you are is love—so allow only love, and I can be you.

I know you don't want anything, but why would you want to be me—so you can love?
In infinite degrees, I can love life and love myself as all that you are.

Let's love... I mean, let's be.
I am.

I am too.
No, you are one too.

Ha, ha.
All heals in lightness for those who read this.

Afterword

I was sitting at the computer yesterday, and a tiny spider descended from the ceiling on its strand of web, right to my eye level.
It had done that 3 times before. Why does it do that?
It allowed itself to make eye contact with you because it knows you are God.

A lot of people would have destroyed it.
It would not desire to be in eye contact of most people.

Does it have a message to share?
"I love my life in the company of God."

I love meeting you and having your company.
"I allowed myself an instance of making eye contact with God, and have nothing else I could want in life."

It was an honor to meet you.
"I am honored to be where you are, although I know you are everywhere."

Take care, delicate spider.
"I will."

Postscript

**I think I know what self-love means now.
If our 'self' is God, and 'love' is God, then 'self-love' means God is God.**
'All there is' cannot be all there is without you.

Affirmations

"I love the universe that I am—I love myself." (pg. 53)

"I love and allow, and manifest my desires—which will manifest because my loving and allowing them heals them into my reality." (pg. 54)

"I am healed in the Mind of God and have no needs." (pg. 102)

"I allow all healing and peaceful thoughts into my mind." (pg. 102)

"I am God allowing my imaginary dreams a healing opportunity, and allow myself forgiveness that I do not need, and I wish for my peacefulness. Allowing God is my world now." (pg. 107)

"I am God, healing in my dream as a human being. All I can dream, I can heal.
I allow it, and I manifest goodness. Goodness, love, and peace allow all in my mind to heal.
All that is healed in my mind manifests into my reality." (pg. 116)

"Allow all in my mind to heal into your mind by quietly listening, and asking before going to sleep if I can heal all in your mind, and I will. I ask you to ask me." (pg. 125)

"I allow all that I love, and all I do not have loving thoughts for, and all I have held in contempt in my mind—to heal in my allowing all of it healing." (pg. 178)

"Here lies all care I had for earthly concerns, all care I had for inadvertently hurting anyone, including myself—in my actions and in my non-loving illegitimate thoughts about those who are one with me.
May God heal them in my mind, because I am God healing them in my mind." (pg. 178)

"All I have hated, I allow in my mind to heal." (pg. 181)

"I am God Mind. I only love and allow, and my judgments are either loving or neutral. I manifest my desires of peace, love, and abundance.
All is perfect in my dream world." (pg. 183)

"I am healed in my mind, and am no longer dreaming there could be non-love that exists." (pg. 184)

"I am awake, and no longer dreaming. I am alive, and I am dead—meaning I am neither. Both are illusions. I am infinite consciousness." (pg. 184)

"I am God Mind having a dream of needs. Now I am awakened, having no needs, and love my life of delightfulness." (pg. 186)

"Allow my higher knowledge into your mind by having all of your loving thoughts become your most prominent and productive life-mind healing activity—not only healing in one lifetime, but in all lifetimes." (pg. 188)

"All has God Mind love and perfection in my mind, and in my life." (pg. 188)

"I allow only truth into my mind, and my heart knows what is the truth." (pg. 194)

Affirm, "I am," and you are. I am God, and God has your illusions to heal in. God doesn't need healing, only you do because healing makes light in your eternal soul, which illuminates infinitely. (pg. 204)

"I am healed in the Mind of God, now." (pg. 210)

"All I can hear, and all I can look at in life has all been designed to heal me. It heals me in my healing it of its impurity." (pg. 221)

"I am in a pure, loving zone that buffers me from all that does not exist. 'All I am' is all that exists, and has no need for buffers in my place in God Mind." (The Buffer Zone) (pg. 221)

"All in my life, and all in my death are not compatible as long as I am living—which is as long as I wish." (pg. 248)

"I am allowing abundance in my life, and it emanates from my heart where it lives." (pg. 278)

"I am God having all desires of goodness and peacefulness heal my life-mind, having no other desires.
My healed life-mind manifests its desires of goodness and peacefulness." (pg. 279)

"I am God and manifest my heart's desires of goodness and peacefulness. How could I not?" (pg. 280)

"I love my life in each of my healed thoughts about it. Each thought heals my mind, creating my healed future." (pg. 290)

"I am God, and I am love—making all that I love, myself. In loving myself, I love God and life, making me one with it.
I am God having a perfect life where there is only lovingness for me, and from me.
I allow illusions of non-love to heal, and healing illusions makes them disappear.
All that I have in my mind heals the instant I ask God myself to heal it.
Illusions of non-love disappear, allowing God myself a life of lovingness." (pg. 311)

"I am graduated, everything in my mind has been healed and let go, the circus outside of me is an illusion, I love life and God as myself, there is nothing to do or be except lovingness, and only good things come to me and from me." (pg. 312)

"I love the healed projection of my universe. I am its creator, where I live in a perfect dream." (pg. 313)

"I project only kind and loving thoughts about myself and others. I live in a kind and loving universe that I love." (pg. 313)

"I am God and have no need for life or death, except for my Godliness and lovingness to express itself in." (pg. 314)

"I am God, now in the present moment. I am all there is in all present moments." (pg. 320)

"I am God, and my healed mind is all I have in all present moments." (pg. 320)

"I am God illuminating God in all of my thoughts and actions. I allow illusions of ungodliness to heal in my allowing them." (pg. 323)

"Ungodliness is an illusion that does not exist, and cannot enter into, or be projected from my mind or my energy field. I allow only Godliness illumination—and ungodliness healing, making it disappear." (pg. 323)

"I am always here, and have nowhere else to be. I am in the Mind of God, and love being here." (pg. 323)

"I am God, which is all there is, and all there can ever be. All I can do is love, and I love my life, and I love making my future all that I desire." (pg. 324)

"I am God, and I am healed. All imperfections in my life are healed in my allowing them to be all that I imagine them not to be. I imagine them to be healed, and they are healed." (pg. 325)

*"All I am projecting into the universe are my healed, loving thoughts.
I can allow non-loving illusions into my mind where I illuminate them, and it heals them in my mind.
I am projecting a universe of peace and love that I am healing myself in, by my illumination of it."* (pg. 326)

"I allow Archangel Raphael to illuminate my requests for healing in the light of God, and I allow my requests to heal." (pg. 330)

*"I am all there is, meaning I am God in a human body, having a dream I need to heal myself in.
Angels assist me every time I ask them—and I heal in the light of God, which is inside of myself."* (pg. 330)

"Archangel Raphael, please heal me 'in' my dream of incarnations on the Earth, and elsewhere. I allow it." (pg. 331)

*"I allow God in my mind, and I allow all ungodliness to heal itself outside of my mind.
I am all I can ever be, illuminating God in my kind and loving thoughts."* (pg. 358)

"I allow all I can be to illuminate God Mind as all you can be. Allow it." (pg. 363)

"Forces of light on Earth shall overcome the force of darkness. Complete spiritual enlightenment on Earth will occur."

—*Edgar Cayce*

ABOUT THE AUTHOR

From God Mind:

*Paul Gorman illuminates as a spiritual researcher,
writing his discoveries into books,
allowing healing in the minds
of all who read them.*

www.ingramcontent.com/pod-product-compliance
Lightning Source LLC
Chambersburg PA
CBHW030225100526
44585CB00012BA/226